PROJECT CHECO REPORT
Contemporary Historical Evaluation of Combat Operations

ASSAULT AIRLIFT OPERATIONS

23 FEBRUARY 1967

HQ PACAF
Directorate, Tactical Evaluation
CHECO Division

Prepared by:
Lt. Col. B. A. Whitaker and Mr. L. E. Paterson

S.E. Asia Team

This document is classified SECRET in accordance with AFR 205-1.

WARNING

This document contains information affecting the security of the United States within the meaning of the Espionage Laws, Title 18, U.S. Code 793 and 794. Transmission or revelation of its contents in any manner to an unauthorized person is prohibited by law.

The material within this report is to be treated with the utmost discretion. Under no circumstances shall possession thereof, or the information contained therein, be given to any personnel other than those whose duties specifically require knowledge thereof. Information required in the performance of his duties.

Retain or destroy in accordance with AFR 205-1. Do not return.

DISTRIBUTION

HQ USAF

AFAMA	1 Cy	AFSMS	1 Cy
AFBSA	1 Cy	AFSLP	1 Cy
AFCHO	2 Cys	AFSTP	1 Cy
AFFRA	1 Cy	AFXDOD	1 Cy
AFGOA	2 Cys	AFXDOL	1 Cy
AFIGO	1 Cy	AFXOP	1 Cy
AFIIN	1 Cy	AFXOPFA	1 Cy
AFISL	1 Cy	AFXOPFL	1 Cy
AFIAS	1 Cy	AFXOPFN	1 Cy
AFNINDE	3 Cys	AFXOPFR	1 Cy
AFNINCC	1 Cy	AFXOPFH	1 Cy
AFNINA	1 Cy	AFXOPFI	1 Cy
AFOMO	1 Cy	AFXPD	9 Cys
AFPDP	1 Cy	AFXDOC	1 Cy
AFRDC	1 Cy	SAFOI	2 Cys
AFRDR	1 Cy	SAFLL	1 Cy
AFRDQ	1 Cy	SAFAA	1 Cy
AFSDC	1 Cy		

AIR UNIVERSITY

ASI-HA	2 Cys	AUL3T-66-7	1 Cy
ASI(Loyal Look)	1 Cy	ACSC	1 Cy

MAJCOM

TAC(DPLPO)	2 Cys	AFSC (SCL)	1 Cy
9 AF	1 Cy	AFLC (MCF)	1 Cy
12 AF (DAMR-C)	1 Cy	ATC (ATXDC)	1 Cy
19 AF (DA-C)	1 Cy	SAC (DCS/I)	1 Cy
USAF SAWC	1 Cy	SAC (DXIH)	1 Cy
USAF TAWC (DA)	1 Cy	SAC (DPL)	1 Cy
USAF TARC	1 Cy	USAFE (OPL)	5 Cys
USAF TALC	1 Cy	USAFSO (NDI)	1 Cy
USAF TFWC (CA)	1 Cy	USAFSO (BIOH)	1 Cy
MAC (MAXDC)	1 Cy		

HQ PACAF

C	1 Cy	IG	1 Cy
DOP	1 Cy	DOIH	1 Cy
DP	1 Cy	5 AF (DOP)	1 Cy
DI	1 Cy	13 AF (DPL)	1 Cy
DO	1 Cy	7 AF (CHECO)	7 Cys
DM	1 Cy	DOPEC	3 Cys
DPL	1 Cy		

FOREWORD

The following report traces the development of the Assault Airlift capability from its inception through June, 1966. Its growth, and the problems associated therewith, including equipment, support, facilities and personnel are discussed.

Operations during the French/Indo China War are briefly covered in the Introduction as well as "interim" operations following the close of that conflict and up to 1 January 1961. From the latter date, forward, the accomplishments of the 315th Air Division in its assault airlift role are more detailed.

To examine the role of assault airlift in Southeast Asia without considering the effects of "out-country", or inter-theater airlift efforts would leave unexplained many of the logistical handicaps under which assault airlift operates today. Hence, the reader will find several references to "out-country" airlift and to organization and control beyond the geographical limits of South Vietnam.

TABLE OF CONTENTS

	Page
FORWARD..	
I. INTRODUCTION..	1
1. The Environment...............................	1
2. Background of Operations......................	3
3. "Interim" Operations..........................	7
4. Summary.......................................	9
II. 1961...	11
1. General.......................................	11
2. Exercises.....................................	12
3. Deployment of Mobility Teams..................	14
III. 1962..	15
1. Farmgate......................................	15
2. Muletrain.....................................	15
3. Fire Brigade..................................	15
4. Joint Airlift Allocation Board................	17
5. Requirements and Operations...................	17
6. Development of Navaids........................	18
7. Assistance to the RVN.........................	19
8. Exercises.....................................	19
9. C-123 Augmentation............................	22
10. First Flare Drops............................	22
11. Deployment to Thailand.......................	23
12. Operations - Aug-Dec.........................	24
13. Flying Hour Accomplishments..................	26
IV. 1963...	27
1. Airfields.....................................	27
2. Exercises.....................................	28
3. Organization of the 315th TCGp (A)............	29
4. Flying Hour Accomplishments (315AD)..........	31
V. 1964..	32
1. Gulf of Tonkin Incident.......................	32
2. Operations....................................	32
3. Operating Conditions..........................	34
4. Increased Requirements........................	36

		Page
5.	Flying Hour Accomplishments (315AD)............	37
6.	Summary of C-123 Operations.....................	38

VI. 1965.. 40

1. General... 40
2. Airlift Systems................................... 40
3. Airlift Pooling Proposals......................... 45
4. Aerial Port System................................ 45
5. Airlift Control................................... 46
6. Employment of Assault Airlift Forces............. 47
7. Miniport Refueling System........................ 50
8. Utilization Rates................................. 54
9. The "600" Flights................................. 54
10. Flying Hour Accomplishments..................... 55
11. Airfields.. 55
12. Operating Conditions............................. 58
13. Airdrop Delivery................................. 62
14. Special Missions................................. 63
15. USAF Airlift Evaluation.......................... 65
16. Summary of Airlift Operations................... 69

VII. 1966... 77

1. Organizational Structure.......................... 77
2. Command and Control............................... 78
3. Requests, Allocations, and Priorities............ 81
4. Command Post and Scheduling Branch............... 84
5. Problem Areas..................................... 89
6. Projected Requirements............................ 93
7. C-123 Activity.................................... 97
8. CV-2 Activity..................................... 98
9. Army CV-2 Activity................................ 98
10. RVN Airfields.................................... 102
11. Aerial Port Concept.............................. 104
12. Procedures for Emergency Airdrop and Airlift... 107
13. Intratheater Aeromedical Evacuation............. 110
14. C-130 Shuttle Activity........................... 112
15. Airlift Aircraft Losses and Battle Damage...... 113
16. Conclusion....................................... 119

GLOSSARY.. 122

FOOTNOTES... 125

LIST OF FIGURES

		Page
Fig. 1	Organization, as of 21 July 1962	16
2	Organization, as of 8 July 1963	30
3	Organization, as of 31 January 1964	33
4	Organization, as of 31 December 1964	39
5	Organization, as of 30 June 1965	41
6	SEA Force Strength vs Airlift Activity	42
7	Photo C-130 Lapes Delivery	57
8	Major Airlifts, 1965	64
9	Pacific Intratheater Airlift System	71
10	PACAF Airlift Forces	72
11	Intratheater Airlift - Flying Hours, 1965	73
12	Airlift Accomplishments, 1965	74
13	Organization, 1965	75-76
14	Organizational Structure	77
15	WTO - MACV Relationships	79
16	SEA Airlift Request Net	80
17	SEA Airlift Aircraft Locations	87
18	SEA Force Strength vs Airlift Activity	88
19	Assault Airlift in Support of Ground Operations, Jan. - Sept., 1966	95
20	Passenger and Cargo Airlift, First Half of 1966	96
21	C-123 Detailed Airlift Activity	98
22	RAAF CV-2 Activity	100
23	Army CV-2 Activity	101
24	C-130 Airfields	103
25	Aerial Port Detachment	105
26	Flares dropped vs Sorties flown	110
27	C-130 Shuttle Activity	114
28	C-130 RVN Shuttle Summary	115
29	C-123 Activity Summary	116
30	Aircraft Losses and Battle Damage	118

CHAPTER I - INTRODUCTION.

1. The Environment

The Republic of Vietnam is approximately 490 nautical miles in length and ranges in width from 35 to 185 nautical miles. Its total area is approximately 34,000 square miles - slightly smaller than the State of Washington.

The terrain of the Mekong Delta, south of Saigon, is low, flat and poorly drained. During the rainy season, the area has been described as "one, large lake." A few miles northeast of Saigon is a forest-covered mountain range, with peaks up to 8,000 feet. This range runs north beyond the 17th parallel. Between these extremes of delta and mountains are coastal plains and jungle-covered plateaus. In many of the jungle areas are found three canopies of growth; a double-layer of brush, bamboo, rattan and broad-leafed evergreens, all topped by a layer of towering hardwoods, six to eight feet in diameter, reaching heights of 150-160 feet.

The climate of South Vietnam is generally typical of that of Southeast Asia - characterized by alternating dry and rainy seasons. In the South, the summer monsoons prevail from June through September. During the winter months it is very dry. In the North, the seasons are reversed.

These natural factors, plus the lack of sufficient suitable airfields, navigational aids, drop zones, and the fact that, for all intent and purpose, the national railroad has ceased its operations, combine to create formidable transportation support problems. Add to this the constant harassment of the road and highway network by the Viet Cong and it becomes readily apparent that movement along ground lines of communication becomes virtually impossible.

Indicative of the effect of the general military situation and the need for airlift and aerial resupply are comments from an officer who served as Air Liaison Officer (ALO) with the II Corps during 1964:[1/]

> "...The ground situation in II Corps deteriorated drastically in the last twelve months. In September, 1964, one could travel by convoy throughout the Corps. Ambushes were few, and generally for harassment purposes only. At present, every major city is isolated by road cuts from its neighbor and to the sea. Major road clear-and-repair operations by from four to six battalions were required to open a specific stretch of highway, and then only for a few days, as the troops were required elsewhere and the VC gained control of the area once again. The last train to reach Qui Nhon from Saigon arrived in late October, 1964. The trip took 26 days because of blown bridges, rail cuts, and ambushes. None has made the trip since. All resupply of II Corps was by sea and air..."

These factors combine to place the major transportation responsibility on assault airlift. A more unfavorable environment for aerial resupply would be difficult to find. If and when the enemy mounts a counter air effort, the task of assault airlift will become considerably more hazardous.

2. <u>Background of Operations</u>

During the seven and one half year French/Indo-China War, which ended 27 July 1954, the U.S. aid to the French consisted of grants and loans of money, military equipment and supplies to a total value of about $2½ billion. This figure represents approximately 31% of the total cost of the war to the West. Although the U.S. was not an active participant in the war and, consequently, had no control over the strategy or missions in which USAF aircraft took part, assistance was rendered the French, with the 315th Air Division (Combat Cargo) being the principal Far East Air Force unit participating.

During the period of USAF assistance in Indo-China (nicknamed IRON AGE), 5 December 1953 to 1 August 1954, a total of 13,714 personnel were airlifted; 21,422 tons of cargo were carried; and USAF pilots amassed 23,035 flying hours. To this not inconsiderable airlift operation can be added the time and effort consumed by the 315th Air Division in the training of 22 French aircrews.

The U.S. Joint Military Mission to Indo-China (O'Daniel Commission) made its preliminary report on 15 July 1953. It recommended, among other things, the French organize their airlift capability along the lines of the USAF's 315th AD and set up a priority system for traffic. It was also recommended that maintenance and supply support be reorganized to increase the operational capacity of available aircraft.

The French desired to have on hand the maximum airlift potential available to move large groups of troops in the shortest possible time and had expressed a preference for the familiar C-47 aircraft. When informed that these were not available in the necessary numbers, the French accepted C-119's. Plans called for the loan of 22 aircraft to the French, with no proviso for USAF dictation of their use. Subsequently, although the prime use remained one of airlift, C-119's were used for napalm drops in the Dien Bien Phu area during March-April of 1954. By the completion of IRON AGE projects on 1 August 1954, three of the C-119's had been destroyed, five sustained major damage and 30 had experienced minor damage. Practically all major damage was caused by 37mm AA fire; small arms fire accounted for most of the minor damage. Flak, in these early days was generally of moderate concentration and, for the most part, no radar controlled.

Foreshadowing the nature of the air war in Vietnam were the conditions at Tourane (Da Nang) Airfield. The surrounding rural areas were under communist domination and nightly engagements were so close to the air base as to present a threat from stray bullets which, on occasion, struck the barracks. One night, tracer bullets were seen striking the runways but, fortunately, no aircraft damage was sustained. Tourane was like an island in an enemy sea. It was at Tourane, on 14 June 1954, that five members of the C-119 detachment (483rd TCW and 8081st Aerial Resupply Unit) were captured by communists while on a swimming party outside the perimeter defenses.

When the heavy traffic for Indo-China started, both the Military Air Transport Service and the 315th Air Division (CC) had only small detachments at Clark AB, Philippines, to handle normal traffic. The French/Indo-China (FIC) commitments, starting in February 1954, required additional traffic personnel. It was decided that MATS would be in charge of the traffic activities at Clark AB, to include loading and off-loading of aircraft, with the 315th having a liaison officer and three airmen comprising its traffic section. Later, on 19 February, three officers and nine airmen assigned TDY from the division terminals provided some augmentation. On 16 April, this latter group was replaced by two officers and 10 airmen, from the 6127th Air Terminal Group units in Korea and Japan, who were scheduled to return to their units by 1 September.

To relieve the limited storage space and congestion at Clark AB, a plan was evolved whereby aircraft from Japan were off-loaded during the day and loaded at night for Indo-China. It was necessary for many traffic people to work double shifts until additional personnel were secured and more storage space was provided. The cargo was broken down as to destinations within Indo-China which obviated the need for men in Indo-China to reload for other destinations.

Some difficulties were experienced in off-loading aircraft in Indo-China during February and March (1954). Several aircraft had been forced to return, with their cargo, to Clark AB, due to the lack of heavy cargo handling equipment in Indo-China. This vital equipment was later furnished by the USAF.

On 22 March, the 315th AD messaged all wings regarding responsibility for unloading 315th AD aircraft in Indo-China. At Cat-Bi and Tourane airfields, the responsibility rested with the 6424th Air Depot Wing; at other bases, the French (through CHMAAG) were responsible.

The 315th Air Division (CC) and its 6481st Medical Air Evacuation Group became heavily involved in Operation WOUNDED WARRIOR, commencing 26 June 1954. This operation involved the airlift of 502 wounded French soldiers from Indo-China to France, and was accomplished with full medical crews being furnished for each flight by the 6481st MAEG, utilizing organic equipment.

Logistical support of the Indo-China activities suffered, along with other functions, from the "on-and-off" nature of the operations. Since the USAF was merely furnishing aid at the request of another country, it was impossible to plan logistically or otherwise. No one could provide the answer as to "when, or if" the aid would be cancelled or expanded. This situation precluded setting up any permanent type of supply or maintenance system.

Most of the 315th Air Division units participating were involved in special flights which presented no extraordinary logistical problems. The 483rd TCW loaned aircraft and maintained a number of personnel within the theater of operations; the net result was that the 483rd TCW received most of its logistical support from its home base, in Japan - some 2,400 miles away. Although this distance, in itself, created problems, the unit was at least able to preserve its logistical capacity at home base. 2/

3. "Interim" Operations

The seven and one half year old war in Indo-China ended in a truce signed on 21 July 1954, at Geneva, Switzerland, with the official end of hostilities set for 0700 hours, 27 July.

During the ensuing period, up to 1962, the 315th Air Division pursued its mission of providing airlift to elements of the Pacific Command and the United Nations Command. Operations were directed from its Headquarters at Tachikawa Air Base, Japan, and included:

    a. Air movement of personnel, supplies and equipment into prepared and unprepared landing areas by aircraft landings and aerial drops during joint airborne operations.

    b. Aerial resupply and routine airlift of supplies.

    c. Preparation of Air Force cargo for delivery by parachute of free drop.

    d. Evacuation of casualities, personnel and materials.

    e. Exercise of operational control and supervision of commercial air carriers augmenting the Division's air fleet under contract.

f. Air terminal operations.

   g. Special air missions.

Operational control was exercised by the 315th Air Division under a concept of theater airlift operations originated during the Korean War and proven by years of experience, whereby all airlift forces within the theater were controlled by a single airlift-commander, responsible directly to the theater commander. Control by the theater commander was exercised through a board, designated as the Japan/Korea Area Joint Military Transportation Board (JMTB), located at Fuchu Air Station, Japan. The board accepted requirements for intra-theater airlift from area component commanders, matched them against airlift capabilities reported to the board by the 315th Air Division, assigned priorities and allocated available airlift. Airlift requirements were accomplished by the 315th AD upon direction of the Japan/Korea Area JMTB. The latter processed, and the Division accomplished, airlift requests from the entire PACOM area.

Airlift capabilities reported to the board by the 315th Air Division were derived from three sources:

   a. C-124 and C-54 flying hours allocated to the 1503rd Air Transport Wing by Western Transport Air Force (WESTAF), MATS, and further allocated to the 315th AD.

   b. C-54 and C-130 flying hours allocated to the 315th AD by PACAF, after deduction of necessary hours for route support and training.

   c. C-46 and/or DC-4 flying hours made available by USAF contract with Air America, Inc.

As is true of most "cold war" periods, dramatic or sudden growth in either demands or capabilities was not in evidence in this interregnum. It was with steady, measured progress the 315th Air Division pursued its mission until New Year's Eve 1960-61 when the deteriorating Laotian situation placed the 315th in Defcon Status 3, where it remained throughout 1961, with no special operations being conducted or alerts received.

This is not to imply any reduction in 315th effectiveness or accomplishment. During 1961, the 315th Air Division (Combat Cargo) was responsible for the airlift of 172,778 passengers, 4,573 medical evacuees, and 25,983 tons of cargo. Against programmed flying time of 59,091 hours the 315th actually flew 56,866.

4. **Summary**

Assault airlift has been described as the backbone of the in-country logistic effort of the conflict in Vietnam. Its role in the remainder of Southeast Asia is equally important.

The term "assault airlift" is used to identify tactical troop carrier and aerial resupply operations, and to emphasize the combat role of airlift forces. The mission of assault airlift as it pertains to U.S. Army support, is the "retail" delivery of personnel and equipment as far toward the forward areas as possible, using all available Air Force transport aircraft, and the most ingenious tactics and techniques.

In addition to the hostile environment, of primary consideration is the 8,000 nautical mile pipeline for personnel and supplies coming from the CONUS to South Vietnam. The resulting congestion at harbors and airfields has created, and continues to create, serious interface problems between the strategic airlift, surface transport, and the "retail delivery" airlift to the using agencies.

It is hoped this introduction will provide an understanding and appreciation of the magnitude of assault airlift problems in Southeast Asia.

CHAPTER II - 1961.

1. **General**

The 315th Air Division opened calendar year 1961 with a maximum effort application of its capabilities to establish an airlift function and structure which, on a moment's notice, could airlift the many tons of supplies and troops from Japan, Okinawa and the Philippines through Bangkok into Laos or Northern Thailand. The political situation in Southeast Asia had alerted U.S. military forces and it could be the job of the 315th to move these Army, Air Force and Marine units.

Being under Defcon 2, the Division curtailed training missions, remanned the CALSU and MCC structure, and stood-down aircraft. The remanning of the Combat Airlift Support Unit (CALSU) at Clark AB, Philippines, occurred on 2 January. The following day, the C-130 CASF support arrived from the United States. Commitment rates were raised - the Division was ready.

On 6 January, the tension eased with Defcon 3 being reestablished the next day. Shortly thereafter, the bulk of the CALSU and MCC personnel were returned to their home bases.

Following the alert condition, the Division returned to its "normal" airlift role and participated in several significant exercises. These exercises came in unusual magnitude and remarkable frequency and involved the 315th in the deployment and recovery of

8,362 passengers and 4,289,856 pounds of cargo. Delivery by parachute
and airlanding was accomplished under tactical conditions requiring
the employment of the many demanding techniques embodied in Troop
Carrier Doctrine. The division was responsible for the continuous
or intermittent operation of several advanced operating echelons;
for the establishment of aerial ports, communications detachments
and maintenance units to widely dispersed sites; for the organization
and operation of aeromedical facilities in support of deployed commands;
and for the control of all airlift and logistical support activities. 3/

2. Exercises

Among the air mobility exercises contributing materially to
the combat effectiveness of various U.S. and Allied conventional and
special warfare forces stationed throughout Southeast Asia, the
following were especially noteworthy:

   Exercise LONG PASS..... 15-28 Feb 1961
   Exercise AIR BULL...... 20 Feb-31 Mar 1961
   Exercise RAJATA........ Apr-May 1961
   Exercise JAE IL IMNIDA. 26-29 Jun 1961

In the course of these exercises, the 315th executed weather
penetrations, utilized primitive staging facilities, conducted
sustained air-drop and aerial resupply operations with only the most
elementary maintenance and logistical support, and proved the
Division's ability to coordinate and support the rapid combat
deployment of fighting forces, with immediate response and flexibility. 4/

Three additional exercises, in which assault airlift played the stellar role, during 1961 were: Exercise TIEN BING (18 Sept - 5 Oct 1961), Exercise DRAGON FLY (4-7 September 1961), and Project BAYONET (3-4 October 1961).

The largest of the exercises, TIEN BING, involved deploying elements of the 2d Airborne Battle Group (ABG) from Naha and Kadena Air Bases, Okinawa, to Ping Tung Air Base, Taiwan. The following statistics reveal the size of the operation:

```
Aerial Deliveries:   Personnel Dropped... 460
                     Cargo airdropped....   7 tons
                     Sorties.............  15
                     Aircraft deployed...  15
Airlandings:         Passengers.......... 486
                     Cargo............... 431 tons
                     Sorties.............  91
                     Aircraft (deploy)...  39
                     Aircraft (retro)....  52
Combat Control Teams: 5 jumps totalling 884 personnel.
```

During Exercise DRAGON FLY approximately 550 Army personnel and 814 tons of cargo were loaded and off-loaded at each of two sites; approximately 70 air landings and aircraft sorties were made; a total of eight C-124 and six C-130 aircraft were used, with the C-124 flying 50 missions and the C-130 flying 20.

During Project BAYONET, approximately 1708 Army passengers were loaded and off-loaded. This operation took place at Kimpo AB, Korea, and was accomplished with six C-118's, six C-121's and three C-135 aircraft. These flights from Kimpo AB were to Travis AFB, Calif., Fort Knox, Ky, Fort Riley, Kans, Fort Gordon, Ga, and Fort Carson Colo.

3. **Deployment of Mobility Teams**

　　Increased hostilities in Southeast Asia made it necessary to place certain organizations on an alert status during October. This condition remained until December, during which time mobility teams were deployed to Da Nang and Tan Son Nhut, South Vietnam. 5/

CHAPTER III - 1962.

1. FARM GATE

The total airlift capability in Vietnam, as of 1 January, consisted of 32 C-47's of the VNAF 1st Transport Group, at Tan Son Nhut AB, and four USAF SC-47's operated by FARM GATE (a USAF advisory function) at Bien Hoa AB, Republic of Vietnam (RVN). Until this time, supplies, equipment and personnel were delivered inter-theater by the Military Air Transport Service (MATS), 315th Air Division aircraft and U.S. surface transportation. Subsequent internal distribution ("retail deliver") was accomplished by the VNAF aircraft. 6/

2. MULE TRAIN

To assist and complement the VNAF, a C-123 squadron was deployed TDY to South Vietnam on 2 January 1962. Operating under the code name MULE TRAIN, the squadron flew its first mission from Saigon's commercial airfield, Tan Son Nhut, on 3 January, furnishing combat airlift support to the Vietnamese (ARVN) forces. A secondary mission was to provide airlift logistical support to the 2d ADVON and other U.S. units in Southeast Asia.

3. FIRE BRIGADE

In addition to providing normal airborne and resupply of the ARVN, the USAF C-123's from MULE TRAIN squadron, C-47's of the Vietnamese Air Force (VNAF) and U.S. Army CV-2 Caribous, made up a fast-reaction, composite force known as FIRE BRIGADE, which was

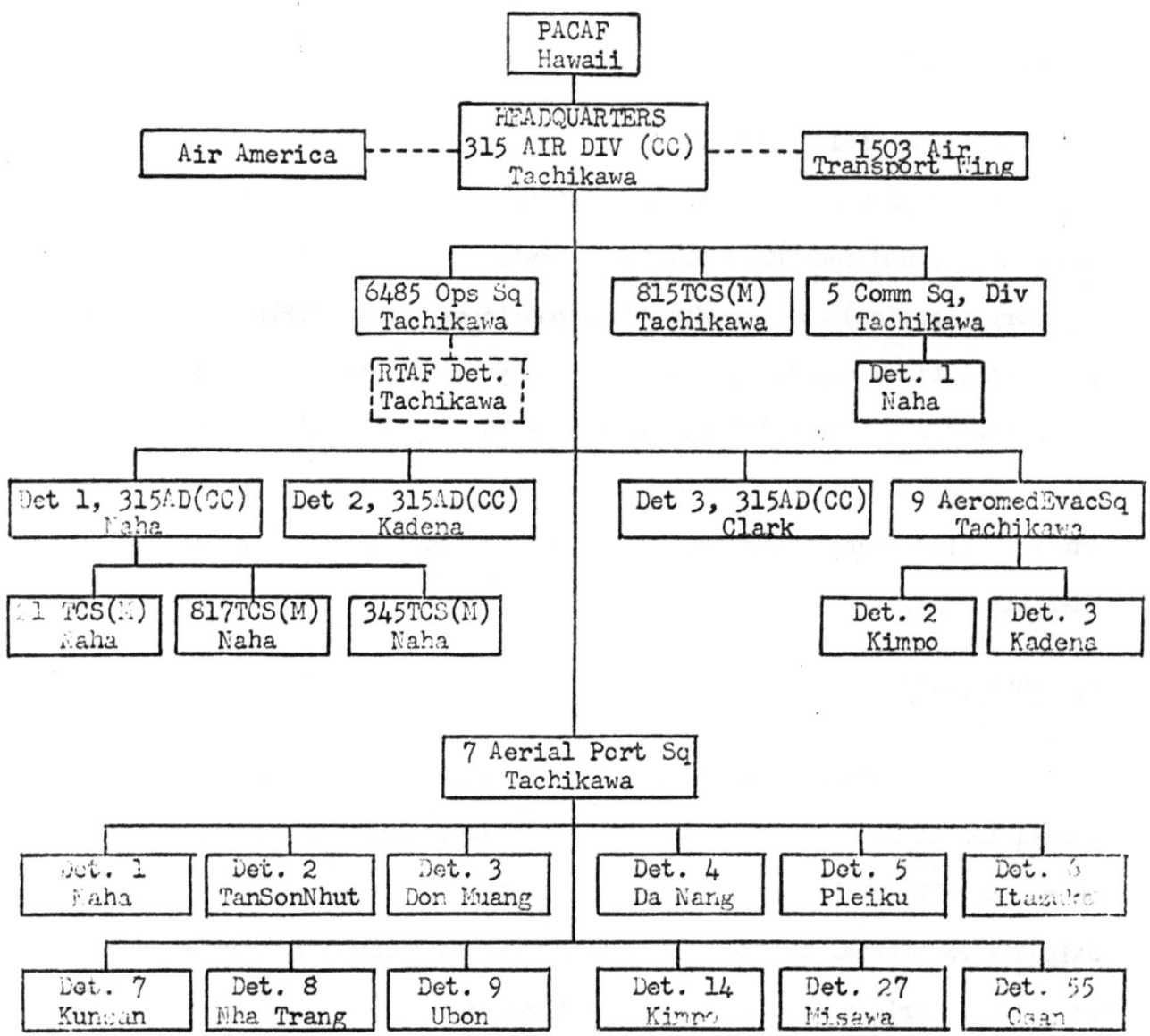

ORGANIZATION

(As of 20 July 1962)

Fig. 1

conceived early in 1962. The operating force was composed of five C-123's, five C-47's and one L-19, with a 30-minute alert status maintained by 500 airborne troops around-the-clock.

The FIRE BRIGADE mission was to support an ARVN or outpost undergoing VC attack. This operation had the highest priority in South Vietnam. As long as there was an aircraft in commission in the RVN, Special Forces requirements were met. Special Forces had established a requirement for approximately 40,000 pounds of cargo per month to be airlanded or airdropped in isolated areas. In practice, this requirement was normally supported by three C-123's, standing 30-minute alert, and two C-47's of the 1st Air Commando Squadron (VNAF). 7/

4. Joint Airlift Allocation Board

Shortly after the arrival of the first C-123 squadron, CINCPAC directed the establishment of a Joint Airlift Allocation Board (JAAB), to effect coordination, allocation and priorities of users. Airlift Traffic Coordination (ATCO) was provided by the USAF, with U.S. Navy and U.S. Army representation.

5. Requirements and Operations

Concurrent with the arrival and initial operation of MULE TRAIN's C-123's, theater airlift requirements increased, resulting in very little average change of effort by the VNAF transport squadrons. Increasing tactical operations by the ARVN, combined with expanding logistical airlift requirements, generated a requirement for flying hours and sorties exceeding the capability of the original 16-aircraft element of MULE TRAIN.

Combat operations were conducted to provide training for combat control teams of the 7th Aerial Port Squadron, 315th Air Division, as well as Division air crews. They also provided paradrop training for the U.S. Army's 549th Quartermaster Company, 1st Special Forces Group and the 503rd Infantry Combat Team.

Unit movements included the positioning of a Division Combat Airlift Support (CALSU) and Movement Control Centers (MCC's).

Combat operations (excluding Det. 1, 315th AD) consisted of 14,077 personnel transported, 606 personnel airdropped, 5,508 tons of cargo transported, of which 98 tons were flown in 1,477 flights expending 5,274 hours of flying time.

6. Development of Navaids

Four radar reflectors were installed at Tachikawa AB, Japan, on a temporary basis as an experiment to gain an acceptable pattern of radar - i.e., returns for airborne radar approaches to a base with 300 feet and one-mile weather conditions during periods of electronic harassment. Repositioning was made during the period to find the most acceptable pattern.

Four radar reflectors were shipped to Okinawa for use by Det. 1, 315th AD, crews at the Yontan Drop Zone. In March, these four reflectors and two from Tachikawa AB were utilized for the first time in an exercise. During Exercise TULUNGAN (10 Mar-3 Apr 1962) they were placed along the San Jose Airstrip, Philippines, in pairs as a navigation aid. Each transport was thereby provided the capability for delivering cargo under adverse weather and enemy electronic harassment conditions.

7. Assistance to the RVN

On 7 December 1961, President Diem of the Republic of Vietnam wrote President Kennedy for aid; immediate U.S. military action resulted, with the initiation of Project BARN DOOR, which was active during the period 3 Jan-16 Feb 1962. During the project, 315th AD C-130's flew 74 sorties, with the C-124's flying 68, to South Vietnam to airlift the Tactical Air Control System (TACS), which was to support tactical air units in South Vietnam. Before execution of the missions, the 315th prepositioned its CALSU and MCC. During the project, the transports flew their special personnel and cargo into airports which were continually threatened by the Viet Cong. Special let-down patterns were developed to minimize the possibility of ground fire. The forward airports had very inadequate navigational aids but, despite this handicap, the plan of operations was implemented in an outstanding manner.

8. Exercises

Exercise GREAT SHELF (28 Jan-16 Feb 1962) was a bilateral air-ground military exercise involving elements of the U.S. Army and units of the Philippine Armed Forces. [8/] Elements of the 2d Airborne

Battle Group and the 503d Infantry Combat Team were airlifted from Okinawa to the Philippines. The training exercises required both air drop and airlanded operations by the troop carrier units. The major aerial delivery mission was conducted on the 6th of February, with a corridor/airlanded mission of similar scale on the following day. Limited logistic airlanded support and aerial delivery resupply missions continued throughout the exercise. Twenty-one C-130 home station departures flew 122 sorties and 28 C-124 home station departures flew 160 sorties. Airdropped were 1,289 personnel and 28 tons of cargo. Excellent aircrew coordination worked to perfection as all drops were on target and injuries to personnel were far below estimates for comparable drops of this size. There was no damage to equipment. Airlanded were 296 personnel and 180 tons of cargo, with the low C-130 offload time of four minutes. Altogether, 2,063 passengers and 430 tons of cargo were offloaded and onloaded in this period of the exercise. The 315th CALSU at Clark AB, Philippines, alone handled a total of 237 arrivals and departures during the course of the exercise (187 in exercise support; 50 in intra-theater airlift support). The Pacific Area flow control responsibility given the 315th AD was handled in an exemplary manner. A primary and effective tool used to accomplish this was a chronological graphic display of special design reflecting all arrivals, on-station times and departures of all airlift to include MATS, 315AD exercise, 315AD intra-theater, MATS TRANSPAC and other types of airlift traffic.

Exercise TULUNGAN (10 Mar - 3 Apr 1962) involved the 315th AD in the airlift deployment of units of the 3d Marine Division to San Jose Airfield, Philippines, and a retrograde of forces following the completion of the exercise. 9/ On 26-27 March, all aircraft departed Okinawa on a five-minute separation corridor and proceeded via airways at assigned blocked altitudes to San Jose Airfield. A corridor flight was made thence to Clark AB and, after refueling, to Okinawa. On 31 March and 1-3 April 1962, C-130 aircraft departed Naha AB and flew to Clark AB, thence to San Jose, reversing the route, and bringing the Marines back to Okinawa. Seventy-five C-130 home station departures flew 181 sorties. During the deployment and retrograde, 1,328 Marines and 200 tons of cargo were moved. TULUNGAN was a bare-strip operation on a single 100-foot wide, 6,000-foot long runway. One battalion, complete with supplies, was moved by 34 aircraft on the first day and an additional battalion with supplies was airlifted by 34 aircraft on the second.

Exercise AIR COBRA (3 Apr - 14 May 1962) was a SEATO tactical air exercise, co-sponsored by Thailand and the U.S. This exercise required the airlift of U.S. forces from bases in Japan, Okinawa, and Clark AB, Philippines, to operating locations in Thailand. In addition, 315th AD was represented by C-130 aircraft and personnel in this exercise. 10/ During the exercise period, limited airlanded resupply was required from Okinawa and Clark AB to and within the objective area. Following the exercise, the deployed forces returned to home stations or originating locations. In AIR COBRA, 90 C-130 airframes flew 377 sorties and 20 C-124 aircraft flew 90 sorties. During final retrograde phase, elements of the 315th AD were placed in an alert status as a result of increased activity in this area.

9. C-123 Augmentation

In May 1962, CINCPAC formally asked the Joint Chiefs of Staff for additional C-123's. As a result of the JCS approval of this request, the 77th Troop Carrier Squadron (TCS) was deployed TDY, in June, from the CONUS (code name SAW BUCK II), bringing the C-123 strength in RVN to 37. (NOTE: SAW BUCK I was the deployment of 16 C-130's from the CONUS to Thailand and the RVN in support of Joint Task Force (JTF) 16, during the Laotian crisis of May 1962.) Both C-123 squadrons were combined into one unit, in September, and designated Tactical Air Force Squadron Provisional Two. 11/ Another C-123 unit was RANCH HAND, a defoliation unit designated Tactical Air Force Squadron Provisional One.

Maintenance of all C-123 aircraft was performed at Clark AB, Philippines, resulting in the loss of approximately 12 flying hours per trip because of ferry time.

10. First Flare Drops

The VNAF C-47's made the first flare drop in February and had the first airborne alert flareship flying on 8 August. Because of a shortage of qualified C-47 pilots in the VNAF, 30 American pilots were assigned to the transport unit for a period of one year. The

VNAF pilots, commanded by Lt Col Nguyen Cao Ky, flew the
aircraft while the Americans taught new techniques of night flare
strike tactics, resupply landing missions on forward dirt strips,
and psywar leaflet and loudspeaker missions. At this time the
C-47 was also being used experimentally to simulate napalm
drops. [12]

11. Deployment to Thailand

Project JTF 116 (14 May-30 Jun 1962) was directed to thwart
the communist threat to Thailand and its neighboring countries. This
project involved the deployment into Central Thailand of Joint Task
Force 116 consisting of Army, Navy, Marine Corps and Air Force units.
Since Laos had lost control of its destiny, the Thai government,
seeing the communists at their border, asked for U.S. support to
stem the threat of entry into their country. The operation took
but a few days and began within hours after the Marine Battalion
Landing Team (BLT) had landed in the harbor of Bangkok. A fleet of
315th AD transports was assembled at Don Muang to onload the BLT.
By using staged flight crews and a large body of operations, maintenance and loading personnel (flown in on earlier aircraft) to
man the terminal end, the aircraft were kept operating around the
clock until the job was done. The main body of the Marine BLT
(461 personnel; 1063 tons of cargo) was moved from Bangkok to Udorn
in 85 successive 315th AD sorties. In an additional 170 sorties,
other Air Force, Army and Navy units of JTF 116 (totaling 976

passengers and 1,867 tons of cargo) were flown from Okinawa and Clark AB to Southeast Asia during the period 14 May-1 June 1962. By the end of June, 3,587 tons of cargo and 2,303 passengers had been moved by air. A commendatory message from CINCPAC, Admiral Felt, to PACAF Commander General O'Donnell, read: "Well done to you and your organization for airlift to Southeast Asia." From Lt Gen Richardson, CJTF 116, Korat, the Division received "Congratulations and thanks for a splendidly executed mission."

During the last week in July and the first week of August 1962, C-130's of the 315th AD and the Composite Air Strike Force, based at Clark AB, Philippines, airlifted Marine Battalion Landing Team 2/3 from Okinawa to Udorn, Thailand; and Marine BLT 3/9 from Udorn to Okinawa. The troops returning to Okinawa were diverted to Clark AB because of Typhoon Nora, which produced 100-mile per hour winds on Okinawa. Except for the two-day weather diversion, the rotational movement met with no problems. 13/

12. Operations - August-December

Exercise GARY OWEN took place in Korea during the period 7-11 August 1962, and was a deployment, tactical supply and retrograde movement of the First Battle Group, 7th Cavalry, in a Phase II Special Mobility Exercise. On this exercise, 900 troops and 1,351,227 pounds of cargo were airlifted without delay or mishap. 14/

During the period 1 September-5 October 1962, the division supported the United Nations resupply of Indonesian guerilla forces remaining in isolated pockets in the jungles of West New Guinea, following the Dutch and Indonesian cease-fire agreement. The division deployed five C-130's, with aerial resupply equipment and a Movement Control Center (MCC), to the two bases of Djarkata and Biak and resupplied forces by airland operations into Kaimana, Sorong and Merauke airstrips. The operation involved flights as long as 2,000 miles over ocean and jungle, and consumed a total of 474 flying and 3,178 aircrew hours. Sixty-three sorties were flown in direct support, hauling 178 tons of supplies and 670 passengers. Forty-four sorties, on which 133 tons and 125 passengers were airlifted, were flown to position, support and return the force. This operation elicited the comment from the Indonesian Air Commodore, Leo Wattimena, that "More good has been done here than the diplomats can do in a long time." 15/

Involving aerial deployment and retrograde of U.S. and Republic of China ground forces, Exercise TIEN BING/SKY SOLDIER II was supported by the 315th AD in October. The exercise was conducted on Taiwan, with U.S. forces deploying from Okinawa. 16/

During the period 6-9 November 1962, C-124's and C-130's supported the air mobility exercise SKY HIGH, conducted by the 1st Battle Group, 17th Infantry, 7th Infantry Division, in Korea. The airlift was conducted in the two phases of deployment and retrograde. 17/

When Guam was devastated by the 184-mile per hour winds of

Typhoon Karen, on 11 November, C-130's and C-124's brought emergency supplies. The first relief aircraft, loaded with 15,000 pounds of food, medicine, communications equipment, tents and relief workers, took off from Clark AB, Philippines, on 13 November. 18/ That same afternoon, another C-130 left Tachikawa AB loaded with 10,000 pounds of radar equipment, relief supplies and personnel. An immediate need was seen for tents to house the homeless populace of the island and over 550 all-purpose tents, weighing over 650 pounds each, were flown in. Relief flights to Guam continued through the end of the year as the stricken island gradually rebuilt and returned to normalcy. 19/

13. **Flying Hour Accomplishments**

	Scheduled Flights	On-Call Missions	Preplanned Missions
DC-4 (Air America)..	4,241 ...	129	
C-46 (Air America)..	2,610 ...	149	
C-54 (6485 Ops Sq)..	2,124 ...	1,130	
C-121 (VR-7)........	3,104 ...	231	
C-124 (1503 ATW)....	6,955 ...	4,998 ...	5,983
C-130 (315AD).......	5,653 ...	3,342 ...	13,696
	24,687	9,979	19,679

During 1962, 199,991 passengers were carried, 41,186 tons of cargo airlifted and 5,612 aeromedical patients were evacuated.

(The organizational structure of the 315th Air Division, as of 20 July 1962, is illustrated on Page 16.)

CHAPTER IV - 1963.

1. Airfields

Military airfields in Vietnam at this time were mere airstrips, with grass, laterite or plain dirt runways. These airfields were completely lacking in security, as practiced by the USAF. Roads crossed runways, pedestrians were allowed complete freedom of movement, vehicular traffic was completely uncontrolled on flight lines and parking aprons. Physical security of the aircraft and crews was hampered by the lack of perimeter fences of even the most rudimentary type. Navigational aids were few or non-existent. Only a relatively few airfields had any navigational aids of any kind, and none of the landing zones or drop zones were equipped with electronic assistance for aircrews. Runways were short, rough, narrow and often with up to a 10-degree slope. Taxiways, if any, were narrow, soft, surrounded by posts, electric poles, vehicle ruts, fences and other hazards. Approaches to the runways often contained obstacles such as trees, fences and even mountain tops. Not infrequently, clearance had to be cut into a hilltop to enable aircraft to operate on the runway of a remote landing area.

Many Special Forces camps could be resupplied only by airdrops, and were totally dependent on airlift for survival. Air traffic control was minimal; only 12 of the airfields had control towers. Operating into these airfields and landing drop zones required crews to exercise the utmost professionalism. Landings and take-offs were frequently made under enemy ground fire and pilots were forced to rely on their personal, immediate knowledge of the day-to-day operations for survival. These pilots were required to judge weather, runway conditions, and to possess an intimate knowledge of the particular area of operation to know if the airfields were suitable and secure enough for them to complete their mission. [20]

Ultimately, because of the aviation buildup of all services and Free World Forces, it became necessary to establish certain minimum criteria at selected airfields to relieve the overburdened civil facilities, but proper equipment was not to be had until much later. [21]

2. Exercises

During 1963, airlift effort was directed to several exercises involving prepositioning, tactical deployment and retrograde of U.S. Army, Marine Corps and Republic of China forces. Two of these training operations, DHANARAJATA/TIDAL WAVE and RUNNING WATER I, directly affected the airlift capability in Southeast Asia. The former, conducted in mid-June 1963, deployed U.S. forces from bases throughout the Far East and Southeast Asia to operating locations in Thailand and tested the capability of Thai airfields to support large-scale airlift. During the TIDAL WAVE phase (build-up) over 50 military air transports saturated various points in Thailand with personnel and cargo from staging areas outside the country in a realistic test of rapid build-up. [22/]

During the period 29 August-4 September 1963, Exercise RUNNING WATER I involved the prepositioning of aircraft for the purpose of possible airlift of forces to protect and evacuate U.S. noncombatants in the Republic of Vietnam and was an excellent test of assault airlift capability in support of contingency plans. During the early phases it was directed that all available C-130 and C-124 aircraft be placed on Okinawa for a lift requirement of 81 loads. When this requirement was reduced to 75 loads, it was possible to release more aircraft to WTO missions. It was during this exercise that all training of PACOM units was suspended, the majority of C-124 and C-130 scheduled and projected flights were cancelled and maintenance schedules disrupted. All delayed airlift was accomplished and normal operation resumed on 11 September. [23/]

3. <u>Organization of the 315th Troop Carrier Group (Assault)</u>

The 315th Troop Carrier Group (Assault), on 3 July 1963, received 51 C-123B aircraft to be assigned to the newly-activated 309th, 310th, and 311th Troop Carrier Squadrons for use in the counterinsurgency warfare in Vietnam. Two of these aircraft suffered crash and hostile fire damage and were dropped from the Air Force inventory; one was attached to the 315th Troop Carrier Group Headquarters; three were on loan to the combat support group.

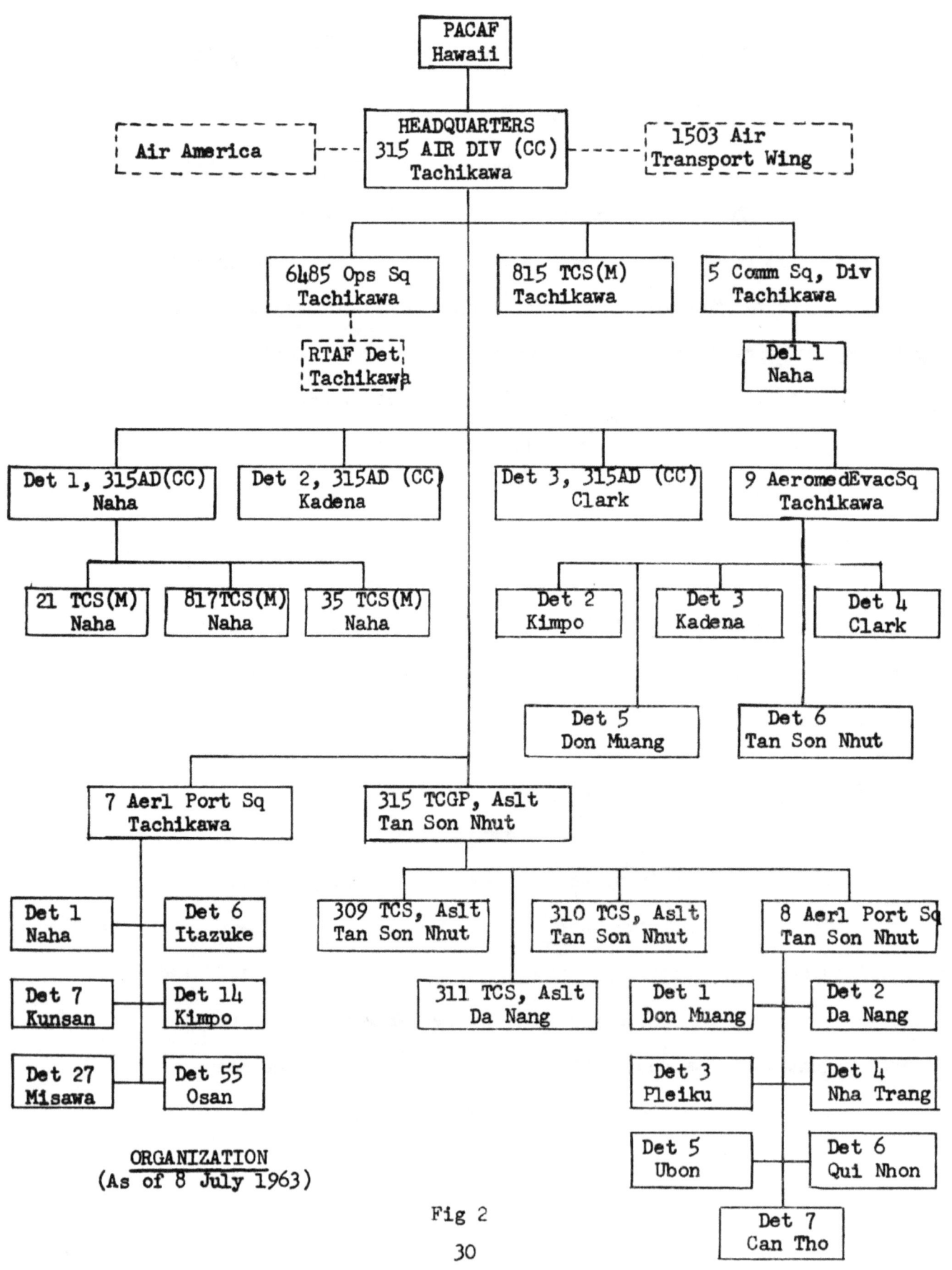

ORGANIZATION
(As of 8 July 1963)

Fig 2

By year's end, the three squadrons of the 315th TCG possessed 45 of the 49 C-123B's authorized.

As noted in Chapter VII, these units and assigned aircraft were under the operational control of the Commander, 2d Air Division, who in turn acted as the Air Force component commander for COMUSMACV. Due to this organizational arrangement, the accomplishments of the 315th TCG are noted separately from those of the 315th AD. 24/ (For organizational structure as of July 1963 refer to Page 30).

	Aircraft			Hours	Poss. Acft Sorties	Pax	Cargo Tons
	Auth	Poss	O/R				
July......	48	45	31	2998	2216	16,373	2884
August....	48	47	31	2582	2088	13,766	3098
September.	48	47	36	2707	2315	13,707	3328
October...	48	48	33	2679	2259	13,794	3342
November..	48	46	37	2852	2512	14,004	3850
December..	48	44	32	3153	2689	16,047	4478
Totals				16,971	14,079	87,691	20,980

4. **Flying Hour Accomplishments (315AD)**

	Scheduled Flights	On-Call Missions	Preplanned Missions
DC-4 (Air America)	3,469	98	
C-46 (Air America)	2,712	112	
C-54 (6485th Ops Sq) ..	2,033	493	14
C-121 (VR-7)	2,889	560	
C-124 (1503 ATW)	6,011	6,511	7,397
C-130 (315AD)	6,320	3,643	11,404
	23,434	11,417	18,815

Scheduled and non-scheduled airlift carried 222,631 passengers, airlifted 46,180 tons of cargo and evacuated 6,527 aeromedical patients during 1963. 25/

CHAPTER V - 1964.

1. Gulf of Tonkin Incident

The deteriorating situation in Southeast Asia, culminating in the Gulf of Tonkin incident on 5 August 1964 with direct contact between the U.S. Navy and North Vietnamese forces, precipitated a limited deployment of U.S. forces to Thailand and South Vietnam. Detachment 3, 315th Air Division, because of its geographical location at Clark AB, Philippines, became immediately involved in the airlift portion of the deployment and functioned as the Movement Control Center (MCC) for the 315th AD intra-theater and Composite Air Strike Forces (CASF) airlift. The division airlift was augmented by three CASF squadrons of the Tactical Air Command (TAC). Two of these squadrons, upon termination of the operation, did not redeploy to the CONUS but remained in place at Clark and Naha to meet future airlift augmentation requirements. (For comparative organization, Jan-Dec 1964, refer to Pages 33 and 39.) Most of the problems encountered during the operation were due to the saturation of Clark AB facilities by the sudden influx of aircraft and personnel. Support of airlift operations and personnel was excellent in view of the host base's limitations. 26/

2. Operations

Scheduled operations consisted of an airline type of operation, regularly transiting specific bases in response to a published schedule. Preplanned and on-call missions were similar, differing only in urgency. A preplanned mission was a special

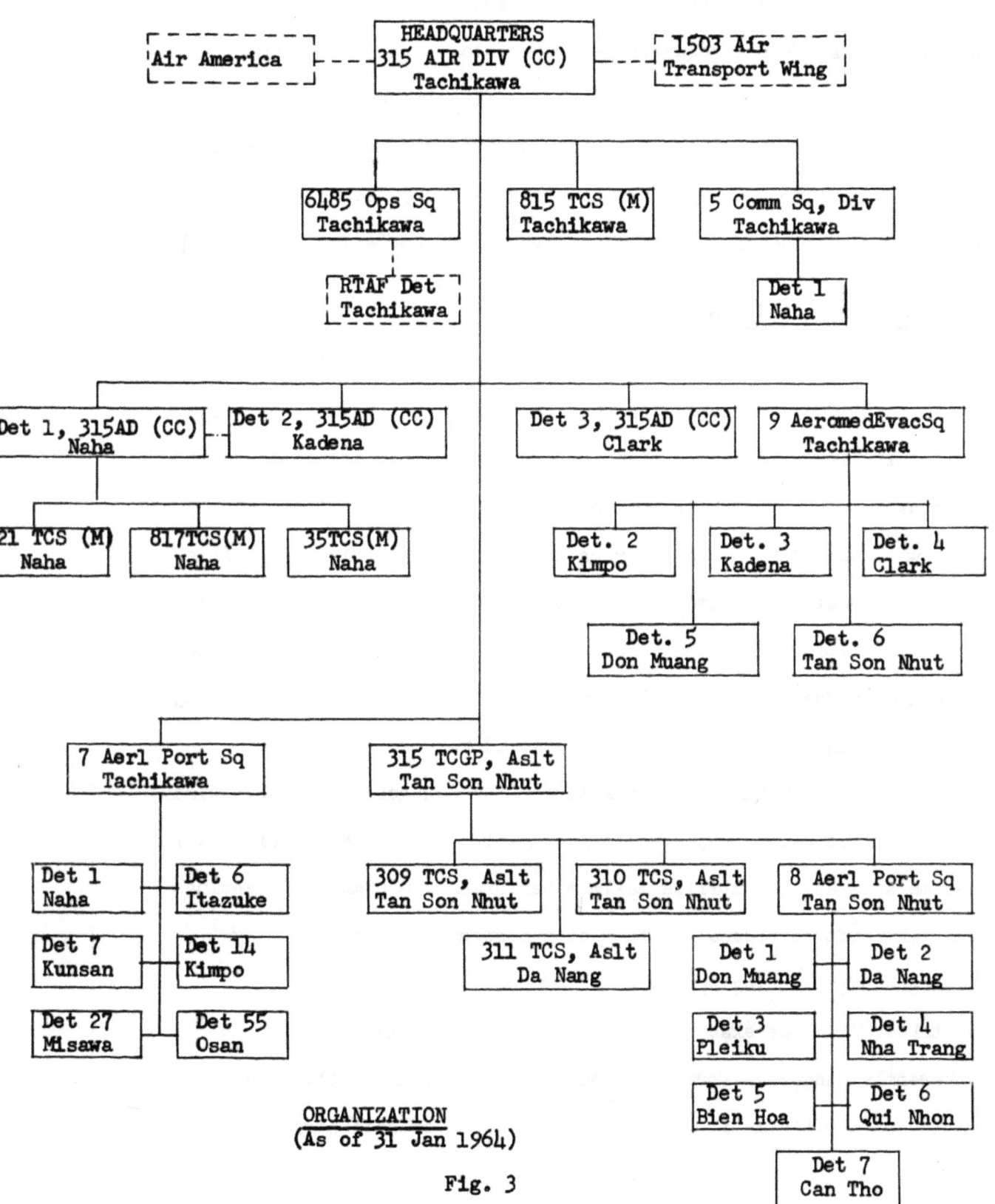

ORGANIZATION
(As of 31 Jan 1964)

Fig. 3

mission airlift committed against a requirement known at least 72 hours in advance of a required delivery date, but not of a continuing nature warranting a schedule. An on-call mission was the same as a preplanned except for the fact that notification was received less than 72 hours in advance of the required delivery date. Airlift priority was as determined by the WESTPAC Transportation Office.

3. Operating Conditions

Aircrews were forced by weather at times to fly underneath the overcast at low altitudes. During the monsoon season, this entailed low-visibility flight conditions through mountain valleys and over formidable ridges. Trying to find a landing field or drop zone, even with the most accurate navigation charts available, was difficult under the best of conditions. An alternate method was "VFR-on-stop" flying, climbing above the clouds after take-off, proceeding to the approximate destination and looking for a "sucker-hole." On finding this break in the clouds, the pilots would make a VFR let-down, attempt to orient and fly to the target through gusty, variable winds, all the while being subjected to ground fire. Through experience, it became advisable to utilize maximum performance/minimum run landings and take-offs to reduce the time of exposure to enemy fire. By flying a high landing approach and by "pulling" the aircraft off on take-off, crews exacted the most from the airplane. While not inherently dangerous from the standpoint of flying safety, these maximums resulted in flying on the outer edge of safe performance.

Engine failure, during any phase of these maximum performance maneuvers, usually resulted in an accident. Any emergency, normally minor in nature, rapidly assumed major proportions in this type of operation.

Flying in Southeast Asia, of necessity, involves rough handling of aircraft off and on semi-improved, soft airfields which, in turn, results in rapidly deteriorating runway surfaces. Aircraft maintenance, particularly landing gear repairs, increases. Main gear tires of the C-130, for example, are ordinarily good for many landings but, under these conditions, must be changed frequently. 27/ Pierced steel planking (PSP) runways tend to curl and break under the heavily loaded aircraft and the plank edges cut tires. On aluminum matting runways (AM-2), one C-124 landing results in the same runway wear as five C-130 landings or 60 C-123 landings. Laterite runways are usually studded with protruding sharp rocks or chuck holes, either of which is hard on landing gears, tires and even gear door fairings.

At all landing areas, parking and loading space was critically short and remains so. At the end of 1964 there were only 14 airfields in Thailand and South Vietnam with runways long enough to permit sustained jet operations. These fields and their runway lengths were: 28/

Don Muang......	8,843 ft.	Ubon............	7,000 ft.
Korat..........	9,845 ft.	Nakhon Phanom...	6,000 ft.
Koke Kathiem...	7,300 ft.	Udorn...........	7,000 ft.
Takhli.........	9,845 ft.	Phitsanulok.....	6,000 ft.
*Tan Son Nhut...	9,960 ft.	*Nha Trang.......	6,000 ft.
*Bien Hoa.......	10,000 ft.	*Qui Nhon........	5,100 ft.
*Da Nang........	10,000 ft.	*Pleiku..........	6,000 ft.

In December 1964, MACV directed the airfields asterisked (*), above, plus Ban Me Thout, Soc Trang, Vung Tau and Quang Ngai, be supplied the following minimum equipment: 29/

> Control tower with UHF/VHF/FM radio.
> Approach control facilities.
> IFR clearance capability.
> Terminal navigation capability.
> Approved instrument approach facility.
> Approved instrument departure.
> Runway lights.
> Crash rescue unit (excluding helicopters).
> Access to a weather facility.

4. Increased Requirements

To point up the increase in airlift requirements, by June 1964 6,623 tons of cargo and passengers were carried in 2,882 sorties. This airlift was accomplished by three squadrons of C-123's, the 1st Air Commando Squadron C-47's at Bien Hoa, two Bristols of the Royal New Zealand Air Force (RNZAF), and various administrative aircraft and out-of-country aircraft which were periodically controlled for use in in-country cargo movement. 30/ Because of this increase in airlift requirements and the diversion of some C-123 aircraft to support the Laos/Thailand operation, MACV asked that the C-123 squadron, being held in reserve in the U.S., be deployed to the RVN.

In the Fall of 1964, floods in Central Vietnam required the majority of the airlift capability be utilized in flood relief. Prior to the floods, about 70 percent of all U.S. and RVN movements were by road, and almost 90 percent of the Vietnamese requirements were satisfied by road LOC's (about 700 tons monthly). The balance was shipped by air (five percent), by rail (five percent) and by sea (20 percent). During and immediately after the floods, only about 20 percent was moved by road; the remainder by sea and air. During this period, some U.S. advisory detachments ran out of food for lack of air delivery. 31/

Transportation requirements during 1964 increased for several reasons: First, U.S. participation reversed from a "Phase-Down" to a buildup; this was typified by the U.S. strength rise from 15,989 to 23,301 by the end of 1964. Second, Free World contingents arrived. Third, VC activity reduced the dependability of land transport. And, fourth, floods resulted in emergency transportation requirements.

Although the Southeast Asia Airlift System (SEAAS) carried 16,727, tons in December 1964, which included augmentation in the system by six Royal Australian Air Force (RAAF) CV-2B Caribous, there was a backlog at year's end. 32/

5. **Flying Hour Accomplishments (315AD)**

	Scheduled Flights	On-Call Missions	Preplanned Missions
DC-4 (Air America)....	3,111	148	
C-46 (Air America)....	2,984	186	
C-54 (6485 Ops Sq)....	1,973	655	239
C-118 (6485 Ops Sq)...	272	131	7
C-121 (VR-7)..........	2,535	390	1,042
C-124 (1503 ATW)......	4,766	3,425	9,916

```
C-130 (Rote Sq).......  1,507 ...  2,109 ...    750
C-130 (315AD).........  6,396 ...  9,548 ... 11,012
                       ------     ------    ------
                       23,544     16,592    22,966
```

Scheduled and non-scheduled airlift carried 203,882 passengers airlifted 51,483 tons of cargo and evacuated 7,896 aeromedical patients during 1964. 33/

6. <u>Summary of C-123 Operations</u>

	Aircraft			Poss. Acft.			Cargo
	Auth	Poss	O/R	Hours	Sorties	Pax	Tons
January...	48	45	36	2793	2478	15,302	3949
February..	48	46	38	2845	2333	15,463	3675
March.....	48	49	39	3290	2868	17,487	4545
April.....	48	51	42	3391	3133	20,085	5043
May.......	48	50	39	3327	2852	17,755	4565
June......	48	51	41	3215	2882	18,119	4703
July......	48	49	48	3412	2947	19,309	3327
August....	48	51	48	3148	2658	15,875	2733
September.	48	51	48	3034	2477	18,424	5761
October...	48	57	48	3198	2791	22,340	6300
November..	64	71	64	3547	2968	14,472	3716
December..	64	67	64	3786	3447	23,540	6037
Totals..........				38,986	33,834	218,171	54,354

Source: PACAF Comptroller Report FY's 1964-65.

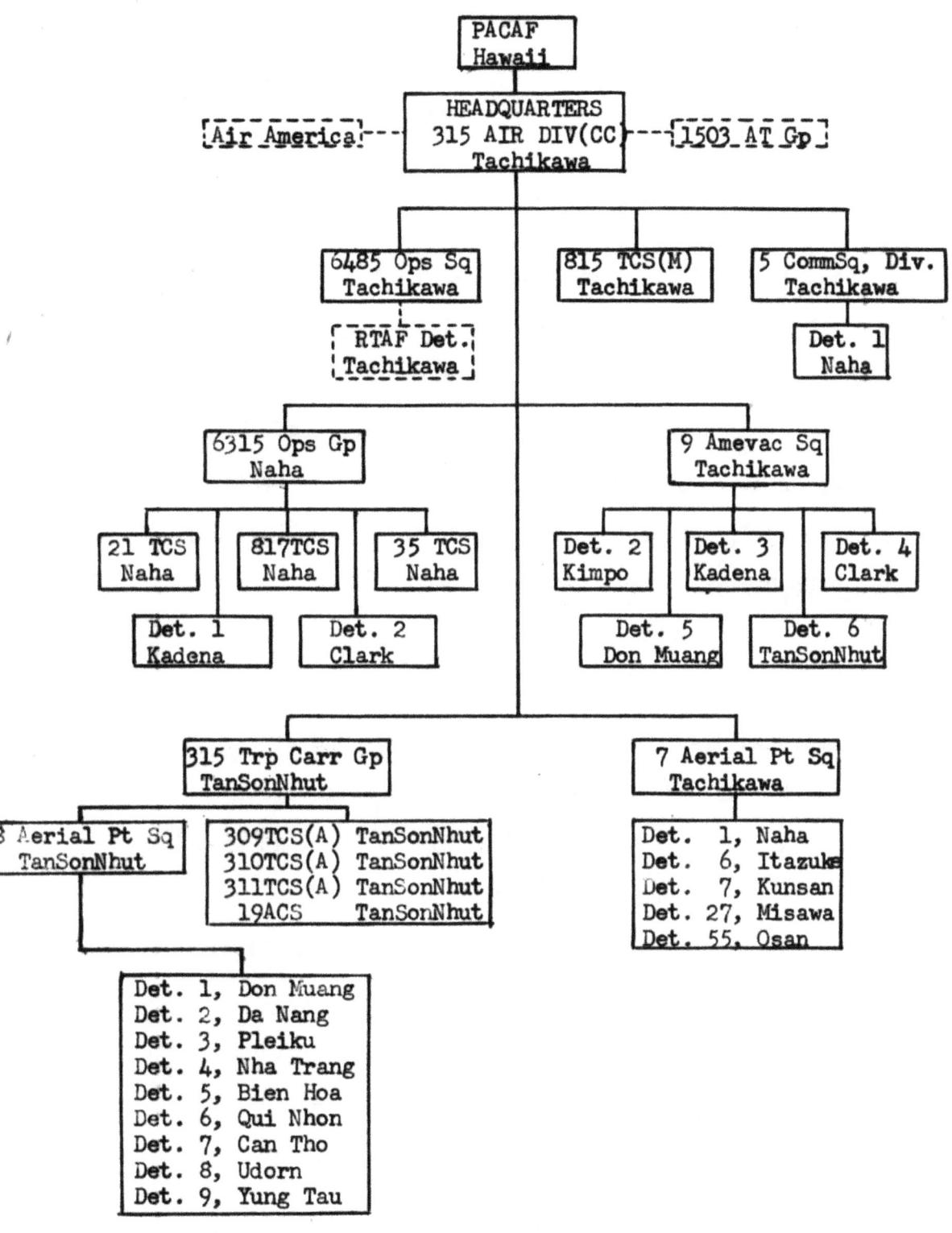

ORGANIZATION
(As of 31 Dec 1964)

Fig. 4

CHAPTER VI - 1965.

1. General

The year 1965 was to note a skyrocketing of airlift statistics - the need for additional airlift resources was clear. The increasing tempo of the Vietnam conflict would see the 315th Air Division committed to what was fast becoming an all-out effort. The Division's C-130 airlift force was to grow to 10 permanently assigned squadrons, plus one TAC augmentation (Rote) squadron under Division control in the Philippines. (Refer to Pages 41 and 75.) The aerial port system would triple, with Division personnel strength rising to 6,142.

2. Airlift Systems

At this time, two distinct airlift systems existed within PACOM; the Intra-Theater and the Southeast Asia Airlift System (SEAAS). The former, supported almost entirely by the C-130 fleet of assigned and attached squadrons and an attached squadron of MATS C-124's, was under the direct operational control of Division Headquarters. All intra-theater airlift was conducted by a system of priorities allocated by the Western Pacific Transportation Office (WTO), a branch of CINCPAC, co-located with Division Headquarters. The system involved all Division airlift, with the exception of the internal operations in Vietnam and Thailand. Aerial port support was provided by the 7th Aerial Port Squadron, headquartered at Tachikawa, and its detachments in Japan, Korea, Okinawa, Republic of China and the Philippines. 34/

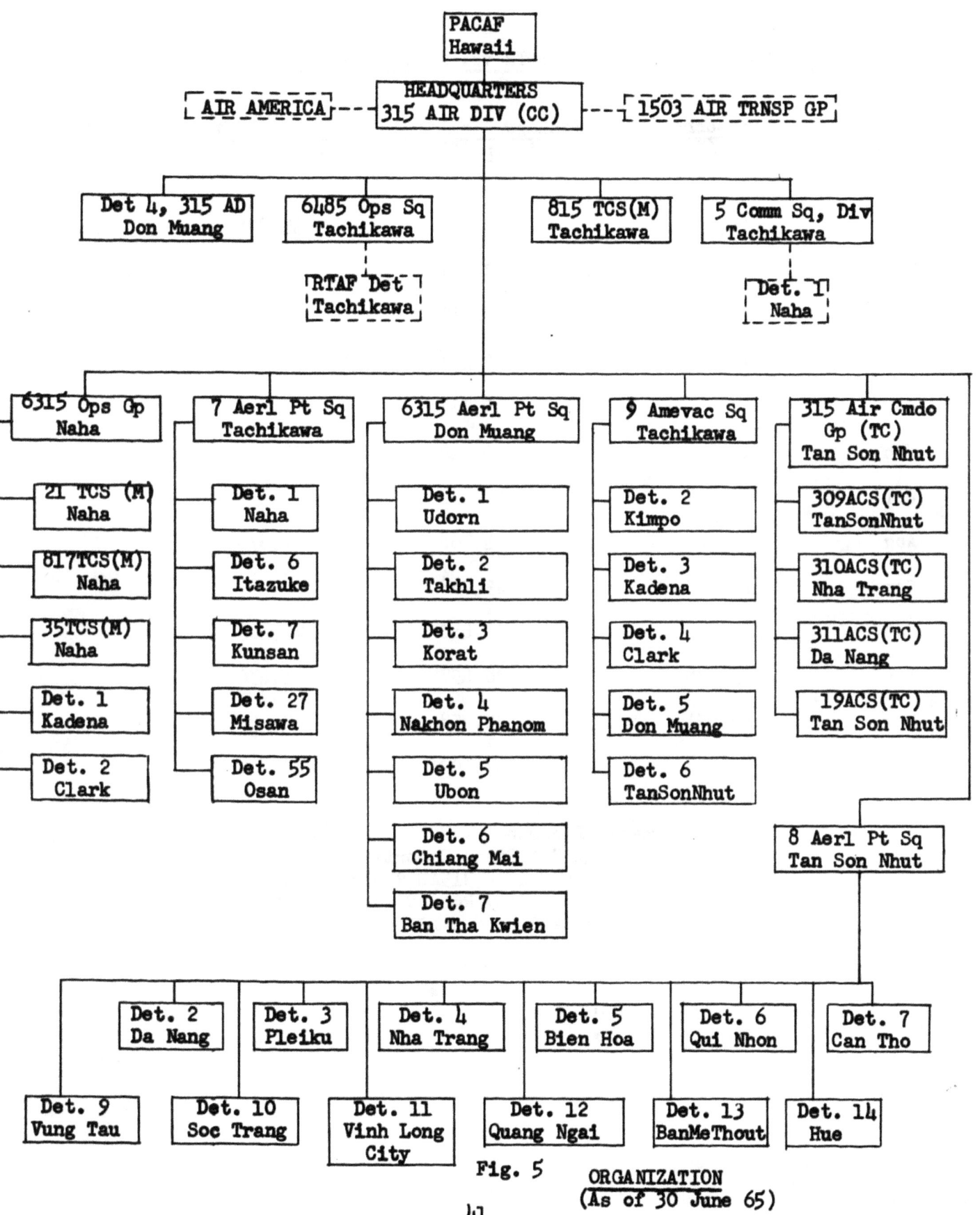

Fig. 5 ORGANIZATION (As of 30 June 65)

SOUTHEAST ASIA FORCE STRENGTH vs. AIRLIFT ACTIVITY

Month (1965)	Personnel in SEA	Tonnage Airlifted Within RVN	PAX Airlifted Within RVN
Jan	28,324	8,122	31,828
Feb	*	7,427	31,602
Mar	*	9,148	34,010
Apr	40,846	9,171	39,268
May	*	9,557	44,936
Jun	69,717	10,248	58,039
Jul	91,777	18,302	72,433
Aug	111,702	24,764	71,870
Sep	144,662	25,768	72,885
Oct	166,721	24,440	82,486
Nov	183,086	28,497	91,476
Dec	198,421	32,258	88,067
		207,702	718,900

Sources: Personnel - USAF Mgt, Summary SEA, & SEA Stat. Reporting OASD (Compt.)
Tonnage - 315AD Report, 8Feb66, & Opnl Acty Rpt (OPSACT), C-123, CV-2 (RAAF) and C-130 acty only.

Fig 6

The Southeast Asia Airlift System (SEAAS) was operated by the Division's 315th Air Commando Group, with headquarters at Tan Son Nhut, AB, Vietnam, (under the operational control of 2AD for COMUSMACV), and involved all of the complex and many-faceted operations within South Vietnam and Thailand. Permanently assigned resources consisted of four squadrons of C-123B's, plus a detachment of six Royal Australian Air Force (RAAF) CV-2B aircraft. An occasional Vietnamese Air Force (VNAF) C-47 augmented the operation. In April, due to a large backlog of cargo in the aerial port system, these forces were augmented by four C-130's of the 315th Air Division in what was intended to be a temporary measure to eliminate the accumulated backlog. By 22 June, due to continued escalation, the C-130 augmentation had increased to nine aircraft, shuttling between bases in Vietnam, and, on 1 July, there were 13 C-130's hauling troops and all types of combat cargo. This was the forerunner of the establishment of a C-130 mission commander at Tan Son Nhut. Centralized supervision of these forces was provided through the 315th Air Commando Group Airlift Control Center (ALCC), which issued daily fragmentary orders in response to airlift mission requirements and priorities established by the Commander, U.S. Military Assistance Command, Vietnam (COMUSMACV or MACV), J-4 Branch.

Of the 13 C-130's available for scheduling by the ALCC, seven were staged at Tan Son Nhut, three at Nha Trang and the remaining three at either Qui Nhon or Vung Tau. The C-130 mission commander formed a C-130 operations section consisting of three officers.

The ALCC made mission assignments to 315AD-approved airfields. Operational control of the aircraft and crews was maintained by the 315th Air Division through the C-130 mission commander. Mission commander elements were later designated at all SEA locations at which C-130 shuttle aircraft were staged.

Although airlift priorities within Vietnam were determined by the MACV J-4 Joint Airlift Allocations Board (JAAB), this board did not operate under ideal conditions because separate airlift request nets and priority establishing boards operated at Da Nang for I Corps and at Nha Trang for U.S. Army Special Forces. This had the undesirable effect of allocating and scheduling from three different locations without optimum coordination. 35/

In September 1965, the mission commander element at Tan Son Nhut was replaced by a Combat Airlift Support Unit (CALSU), manning for which was provided from Division resources, pending approval of additional personnel authorizations. On 8 November the Tan Son Nhut CALSU was redesignated Det. 5, Hq 315th Air Division, and Det. 6 was activated, with station at Cam Ranh Bay, to function as a CALSU. 36/

By December there were more than 30 315th AD C-130's augmenting the SEA airlift system. Aircraft were staged at Tan Son Nhut, Nha Trang, Vung Tau, Cam Ranh Bay, Da Nang and Don Muang. The Da Nang C-130's were assigned to the BARREL ROLL flare mission and did not perform a logistical role.

3. **Airlift Pooling Proposals**

At various times, proposals had been made that VNAF aircraft, Thai transport aircraft, Korean and U.S. Army CV-2B aircraft be incorporated into the SEA airlift system. The pooling of U.S. Army and Air Force transport aircraft for maximum and most efficient utilization was long a subject of controversy, dating back to the "Hump" airlift operations of World War II. The Army maintained that they could get quicker response to tactical emergencies if they controlled their own transports, while the Air Force took the position that airlift could be better managed through a centralized control system. As of 31 December 1965, only the RAAF aircraft were supplementing those of the U.S. Air Force.

4. **Aerial Port System**

On 1 July, the aerial port system in Vietnam consisted of the 8th Aerial Port Squadron at Tan Son Nhut, assigned to the 315th Air Commando Group, and its twelve detachments throughout the country. The escalation of the war so necessitated the expansion of this organization that, by 1 October, the 8th was operating a total of 17 detachments throughout SVN. On 1 December, to further meet the increased demands for aerial port facilities, two new aerial port squadrons were established; the 14th at Cam Ranh Bay and the 15th at Da Nang. Both squadrons were assigned to Division headquarters. 37/

On 15 December, the entire aerial port system in SVN was reorganized and further expanded. Nine detachments of the 8th Aerial

Port Squadron were transferred to the 14th and 15th, and seven new detachments of the 8th were designated and organized. In this realignment action, the 14th absorbed four detachments of the 8th and activated six more, making a total of ten detachments operated by that unit. The 15th Aerial Port Squadron absorbed five of the 8th's detachments and activated seven new ones, for a total of 12 detachments. 38/ Areas of responsibility were as follows:

        8th Aerial Port Sq: III and IV Corps
        14th Aerial Port Sq: Southern II Corps
        15th Aerial Port Sq: I and Northern II Corps

As of 31 December 1965, there was a total of 38 locations in SVN serviced by aerial port squadrons or detachments.

5. **Airlift Control**

Airlift in Thailand was controlled through the 315th Air Division's Detachment 4, at Don Muang (near Bangkok), which was established 10 April 1965. Prior to September, airlift was provided by six C-123's on TDY from the 315th Air Commando Group (ACG). In September, CHWTO authorized the staging of four C-130's from 315 AD resources to Don Muang, freeing the C-123's for return to Vietnam. Management of airlift within Thailand was not as efficient as it should have been as there was no central allocation agency for determining priorities. As many as five users were forwarding requests for airlift direct to the Det. 4 TMC, which in turn published an appropriate frag order for accomplishment of the mission. In addition to this "on-call" type of operation, Det. 4 operated three scheduled flights daily within Thailand. In September, CINCPAC directed establishment of a WTO branch office in Saigon to serve U.S. Forces in Thailand as well as South Vietnam. The tri-service staffed office served as a priority establishing agency and was responsible directly to CHWTO at Tachikawa Air Base, Japan. [39/]

In November, plans were being discussed to move the 463rd Troop Carrier Wing from Mactan, Philippines, to Sattahip, Thailand, at which latter site a new base was under construction. USAF programming documents indicated the 463rd as scheduled to move to Sattahip (south of Bangkok) in July of 1966. [40/]

Aerial port services and facilities were provided by the 315AD's 6315th Aerial Port Squadron (later redesignated the 6th Aerial Port Squadron), headquartered at Don Muang, and its seven detachments throughout Thailand. [41/]

6. Employment of Assault Airlift Forces

Assault airlift aircraft were employed in three major and three special operational categories:

Major	Special
(1) Airlanded assault and resupply.	(1) Defoliation.
(2) Airborne assault and resupply.	(2) Flare support.
(3) Aeromedical evacuation.	(3) Leaflet drop.

The special operations, although vital in nature, pulled aircraft out of the system which would normally have been used for major cargo missions.

In their airlanded and airborne assault and resupply roles, assault airlift aircraft provided air movement of troops and equipment to forward or dispersed bases or drop zones in close proximity to specific combat operations. From the initial phase until completion, they maintained the airlanded or airborne resupply support necessary to sustain operations. Upon termination, the aircraft were frequently employed to reposition the ground forces and equipment to other forward combat or staging areas, as the tactical situation dictated.

Aeromedical evacuation flights were accomplished by means of pre-planned or on-call diversion as the situation demanded and were staffed by the Tachikawa based 9th Aeromedical Evacuation Squadron with its flight nurses, medical technicians and special equipment. This unit furnished aeromedical services on all intratheater evacuation flights. Aircraft support was provided by four C-118's of the 6485th Operations Squadron and by four C-121's of the Navy VR-7 Detachment Alpha. These aircraft were augmented when necessary by 315AD C-130's. On 1 July, the 9th Aeromed was operating five detachments, in addition to its headquarters, at locations in Korea, Okinawa, Philippines, South Vietnam and Thailand. Detachment 7 (Da Nang South Vietnam) was organized on 8 July; on 8 November, the number of detachments was more than doubled when seven additional detachments were organized in Vietnam and Thailand. 42/

Defoliation missions were flown by specially equipped spray

aircraft (RANCH HAND) in response to fragmentary orders issued by the 2AD TACC, upon direction of MACV. On 10 November, the number of specially configured C-123 spray aircraft of the 309th Air Commando Squadron at Tan Son Nhut, was increased from four to seven. Shortly thereafter, the designation of these aircraft was changed to HUC-123B. [43/] Their mission was to spray a chemical defoliant on jungle areas providing hiding places for the enemy. The mission also included the spraying of herbicides for the purpose of destroying VC food crops. Prior to the assignment of the three additional spray aircraft, approximately 250 hours per month were flown by the RANCH HAND defoliation flight. Two aircraft, flying in formation, were fragged daily by the 2AD to perform two sorties each. That the mission was important is borne out by the assignment of the additional aircraft. With the new HUC-123B's it was estimated that future scheduling requirements would consume 600 flying hours per month for the RANCH HAND mission. [44/]

Flare support missions were flown as directed in fragmentary orders issued by the ALCC and were either pre-planned or on-call, as the tactical situation dictated. Commitment to this requirement involved keeping eight C-123's on night alert to aid hamlet defense and to provide illumination for night fighter sorties in South Vietnam. In addition, two C-130's were maintained at all times at Da Nang to provide illumination for the BARREL ROLL and STEEL TIGER missions in Laos, and for the ROLLING THUNDER mission in North Vietnam. [45/] Two C-130 flare aircraft were destroyed on

1 July when the VC attacked Da Nang with mortars and satchel charges. The aircraft were immediately replaced so that almost no degradation of mission capability occurred. It was at this time that operational tests of a locally designed and fabricated flare dispensing unit were successfully completed. 46/

Psywar operations, involving high altitude dropping of leaflets and other types of propaganda materials such as newspapers and toys and candy for children, were conducted by the 315AD C-130 aircraft. FACT SHEET operations involved missions over North Vietnam which took the aircraft and crews directly over hostile territory. (Drops against North Korea were made from high altitudes allowing prevailing winds to carry the leaflets to the target area.) 47/

Other special operations included one electronically configured C-130E aircraft for the purpose of command and control. This aircraft was assigned to the 314th Rote Squadron and was based at Tan Son Nhut under the operational control of the 2d Air Division. Known as the "Talking Bird" it served as an Airborne Battlefield Command and Control Center (ABCCC). At the close of 1965, the requirement for additional aircraft of this type was under evaluation. 48/

7. Miniport Refueling System

Of minor consideration in the over-all assault airlift operation, but nevertheless vital, was the air transport of POL products. On

28 November, two C-130A aircraft were positioned at Tan Son Nhut to fulfill this requirement. The cargo consisted mainly of aviation gasoline and JP-4 fuel for the support aircraft operating out of forward area airfields, and was transported in special bladder tanks carried on 463L pallets. 49/

A requirement had existed for several months to deliver large quantities of aircraft fuel into the Central Highlands of the RVN made inaccessible by enemy forces. Prior to putting the MINIPORT system into service, fuel was flown in by C-130 aircraft, using either 55-gallon drums (65 per aircraft) or 500-gallon rubber drums (7 per aircraft). On and off-loading of fuel from the C-130's, using these methods, was time-consuming and provided less fuel per load than the MINIPORT system (3,500 gallons compared to MINIPORT 4,000 gallons).

Commencing on 28 November, the two C-130's at Tan Son Nhut were each equipped with the 4,000-gallon MINIPORT system. One aircraft being utilized for JP-4 service; the other, 115/145 avgas. Deliveries were made to the following bases: Pleiku (USAF), Nha Trang (USAF), Ban Me Thout (USA), Kontum (USA), Soc Trang (USA) and Camp Holloway, Pleiku (USA).

The following statistics reflect the MINIPORT operation during 28 November-14 January:

	JP-4	115/145 Avgas
Total Flights	71	70
Fuel Delivered	8,000 gals(USAF)	254,000 gals
	278,000 gals(USA)	28,000 gals
Days Fuel Not Deld..	10	13
Avg Daily Dely When Acft Flying	7,526	8,037

Note: MINIPORT maintenance caused interrupted delivery for only one day in JP-4 service; two days in 115/145 avgas service. Most of the remaining down time was for aircraft maintenance.

Refueling vehicles are used in the filling and off-loading operation. Average ground time for off-loading is less than 40 minutes.

On 13 December, responsibility for operation of the MINIPORT system was transferred to the 463d TCW, which was directed to replace the C-130A's with the "B" models. [50/] On 22 December, the C-130 CALSU Commander at Tan Son Nhut submitted a recommendation that the tanker operation be assumed by C-130E model aircraft because of better suitability for the mission. The recommendation read: [51/]

> "1. Currently the C-130 CALSU is providing two C-130B acft bladder configured to transport JP-4 and avgas to satellite air bases to support Army and Air Force small aircraft operations. The maximum capability with one crew per aircraft is four sorties per day at 25,000 pounds of fuel per sortie delivered.
>
> "2. A test has been successfully conducted using the aircraft internal tanks to transport fuel. The concept is as simple as a routine defueling, utilizing an MB-3 power unit and a single point attachment and hose. Although any model C-130 is capable of performing this mission

the additional external tanks make the E model the most desirable tanker vehicle. By employing two C-130E model aircraft an average of 40,000 pounds of fuel can be delivered per each sortie, thereby producing a six-sortie capability with only four flying sorties. Additional advantages accrue: Primarily the entire operation is a great deal safer and cleaner, reducing the dangers of internal spillage and fire in the event of bladder rupture due to hostile fire or malfunction. The requirement to maintain the balky motor pump is alleviated and no extensive or special training is required to qualify the aircraft crews in pumping operations and emergency procedures. Further, the cargo compartment can be utilized for cargo and personnel on both inbound and back haul legs. This bonus feature is not presently available in current configuration. Too, no specific aircraft need be designated as tanker aircraft and lost missions due to NOR tanker aircraft can be avoided by judicious scheduling. A factor of significance to the cost reduction program is the deletion of the entire bladder and pump system.

"3. Other factors to be considered of course are: The acft tank purge requirements prior to accepting avgas for transport. The impact of wear of fuel tank pressure pumps and the landing stressed on the wings with heavy fuel loads. It is our belief that these are considerations which can be readily resolved with appropriate operating procedures.

"4. Recommend the tanker operation be conducted using two C-130E aircraft and 315 Air Div Standardization/Evaluation personnel provide guidance for heavy weight (fuel) operation and that Division POL inspectors provide data on what amount of JP-4 residuals in acft tanks would constitute contamination of 115/145 avgas.

Signed Col Lewis."

On 20 December 1965, the first in-flight C-130 was lost as a result of enemy ground fire. The aircraft crashed and burned approximately five miles south of Tuy Hoa and was carrying a cargo of 26,000 pounds of JP-4 fuel in bladders. The entire crew of five was killed.[52/]

8. Utilization Rates

By the end of 1965, programmed C-130 utilization rates had increased to 2.5 hours daily for A and B models. Utilization rates of the E model increased to 3.0 hours daily, with incremental increases programmed to reach 5.0 hours before FY 67. The increase in utilization rates to obtain increased flying hours and tonnages resulted in greatly increasing the support workload. It demanded augmented aircrew ratios to support the additional flying hours, which in turn produced a need for increased maintenance manhours, generating a requirement for additional maintenance personnel. The increase in tonnage resulted in a heavier workload for aerial port personnel, which also generated a need for increased manpower.[53/]

9. The "600" Flights

On 1 October, as a result of the continuing need for airlift into certain areas, a regular schedule of "600" series flights was begun. These flights, carrying high priority cargo and passengers, provided the aerial port units a more reliable and efficient airlift schedule which improved the in-country airlift. Cargo loads could be pre-planned and passengers offered faster airlift to all air bases. Generally, C-123's were used for airlift within the Corps areas. The longer flights, to bases generating

large volume cargo, were serviced by the C-130. These scheduled
flights continue to be most effective in moving urgent cargo on
a continuing basis and their very existence prevents many individual
short-notice airlift requests. 54/

10. Flying Hour Accomplishments

	Scheduled Flights	On-Call Missions	Preplanned Missions
DC-4 (Air America)	4,557	49	
C-46 (Air America)	2,245	79	
C-54 (6485 Ops Sq)	516	242	113
C-118 (6485 Ops Sq)	2,287	550	143
C-121 (VR-7)	2,400	338	544
C-124 (1503 ATG)	3,031	9,860	1,608
C-130 (Rote Sq)	10,961	23,594	11,199
C-130 (315 AD)	12,848	19,522	9,030
	38,845	54,234	22,637

During 1965, scheduled and non-scheduled airlift passengers totaled 718,900; cargo 207,702 tons; aeromedical evacuation, 5,418 patients.

11. Airfields

During October, the 315th Air Division began to be continually pressed to conduct operations into and out of short and, in many cases, unprepared airstrips in SVN in support of ground forces. The Division was, at first, reluctant to operate C-130's into these fields for obvious reasons of safety and because of the fact that there were few pilots available who were qualified for this type of operation. Also, the load carrying ability of the C-130 would be hampered when operating into these fields because many of the short strips were beyond the capability of heavily loaded aircraft. To use this type of field, maximum loads could not be carried and airlift efficiency, in terms of tonnage, would suffer. However, the capability of the C-130 for this type of operation had been repeatedly proven in CONUS training exercises where unprepared 2,000 foot strips had been successfully used for airland operations. It now became necessary to apply this experience in actual combat operations. 55/

In November, it was decided to operate C-130's into all airfields in Vietnam within the performance limitations of the aircraft. Authority to evaluate and approve such flights was delegated to the CALSU commander at Tan Son Nhut. 56/ Pilots qualified for this type of operation were said to be "short stop" qualified. Minimum runway length for short-stop qualified pilots was fixed at computed ground run distance for landing or takeoff, plus 1,000 feet. On 26 November, PACAF deleted the 1,000 foot planning factor in order to make it possible to operate C-130's into more South Vietnam airfields. Because of the shortage of short-stop qualified pilots, a vigorous training program was established to assure mission accomplishment. 57/ Problems arose in this area because there were no airfields available outside SEA where short-stop training could be conducted. Correspondence between 315AD, 5AF and 313AD revealed that the 313th Air Division did not control any airfields suitable for assault training. The 313 AD suggested that the 6315th Operations Group, at Naha, investigate the possibility of using

several airfields used by Air America for commercial flights. Suggested airfields were Kume Airstrip, Minimi Diato and Miyako Jima. 58/ In November, the Kadena base engineers completed a survey of the airstrip on Ie Shima Island and, as of 31 December, it was this area that held the most promise for C-130 assault or "short stop" training. 59/ Meanwhile, C-130 operations in Vietnam were being increasingly employed using airstrips which previously would not have been considered suitable.

Factors limiting the number of C-130's which could be introduced into the system were: Insecure airfields, limited parking space, on/off-load facilities to include shortages in material handling equipment, and limited messing, billeting and transportation facilities. 60/ Because of short, rough runways, 315AD had restricted C-130 operations to airfields meeting preformance limitations of the aircraft. This normally meant 3,500-foot-runways, but the Commander, Det. 5, 315AD had the authority "in a bona fide emergency" to waive this limitation. He responded by stating "C-130 resources would be applied to max capability." 61/

On 31 October, 2AD asked MACV to "give priority to improve 18 airfields in RVN to accommodate C-130 operations into these fields. Improving these airfields is vitally necessary to increase capability of assault airlift. 62/

12. **Operating Conditions**

Other problems facing assault airlift forces were the hazardous operating conditions and crowded airfields at U.S. Army-controlled sites. In a message to 2AD, CINCPACAF indicated: [63]

> "...Due to the number of near miss incidents between USAF aircraft and Army airplanes...consideration should be given to increased utilization of air drop and aerial extraction delivery to areas or airfields which present unacceptable hazards to safe operations..."

In a letter to MACV in November 1965, 2AD indicated several areas where improvements were needed on forward airstrips to improve the safety of operations. [64] Cited were the uncontrolled vehicles and helicopters on or near the runway and non-delineated taxi-strips, and the need to schedule resupply missions, when possible, during periods when other local air traffic was at a minimum.

During this time, the U.S. Army in Vietnam had in operation or under construction, a large number of 1,500 foot airfields which, although perfectly suitable for CV-2B and helicopter operations, did not satisfy the heavier requirements of C-123 and C-130 aircraft. Attempts were made by PACAF to influence Army planning to include construction of more airfields of up to 3,000 feet length which could accommodate C-130 aircraft. [65]

C-130 operations into the small, laterite, grass, PSP or asphalt surfaced airfields of Vietnam, in addition to being hazardous because of field size, were further inhibited by weather conditions, enemy actions and congestion by Army aircraft.

Haphazard air traffic control by Army personnel and their practice of parking aircraft and stacking cargo so close to the runway that landing and takeoffs for larger aircraft were very dangerous. On 18 December, a C-130 of the 773rd Troop Carrier Squadron was severely damaged on landing when it struck a pallet of 55-gallon drums stacked on the end of the Tuy Hoa runway. [66/] The rough, unprepared runway surfaces at many airfields were taking a heavy toll of aircraft tires because of the presence of large holes and rocks. [67/]

By the end of 1965, the RVN had only 13 adequate and 15 marginal airfields for C-130 operations.

On 12 May 1965, a C-123B, of the 310th Air Commando Squadron, was severely damaged when it landed short at Hon Quan Airstrip, Vietnam. The aircraft carried a five-man crew and, luckily, the accident resulted in no injuries or fatalities. Typical of the environmental conditions under which assault airlift operated, it is felt that the entire description, extracted from the official accident report, is worthy of quote. All assault airlift aircraft operating in the Republic of Vietnam were subject to these conditions: [68/]

> "The airlift mission of the C-123 throughout the Republic of Vietnam is demanding and inherently dangerous. The danger arises not only from hostile actions but from the very nature of the Air Commando Group mission. Marginal weather, minimal airfields, and continuous operation of the aircraft at its maximum performance capabilities, and in some cases beyond, are additional hazards of repeated daily operations which the aircrews meet. The successful completion of each

airlift sortie is of paramount importance. This is particularly true when that sortie is in direct support of tactical ground operations, as this flight was. Airlift operations are conducted from airfields which have none of the refinements possessed by normal operating bases. Many hazards exist which cannot be eliminated because of the demands of combat operations. The Hon Quan airstrip is typical of assault airfields in Vietnam and was the third airfield used to support the Song Be operation. Although it was the least acceptable of the three, the other two airfields were insecure. Additionally, Hon Quan was under unfriendly surveillance at the time of the accident. This field is short, unusable in wet weather and is constructed on a hillside and surrounded by normally unacceptable obstacles. There is no radio contact and field security is normally determined by the presence of a familiar U.S. military vehicle. Still the operational commitments must be met, and this can be accomplished only through a truly professional approach by a highly experienced and qualified individual. This instructor pilot is one of the most experienced in the group and is considered one of the most highly qualified. The assault approach and landing is a precise maneuver designed to utilize the minimum runway length and diminish the effect of hostile ground fire. It is kept as close as possible to the secure field area and normally has a descending final turn. Manifold pressures will vary as required to establish the aircraft on an optimum approach path for the last segment of final. However, inasmuch as assault approach speed is power-off stall plus ten knots, as compared to power-off stall plus thirty knots for normal approaches, the proper power to gross weight ration must be established to insure safe flare and touchdown. The manifold pressure setting of 26 to 28 inches of mercury is considered adequate by the pilot members of the board for the gross weight at the time of the accident. Although this is within design performance capabilities, it is most certainly insufficient to allow recovery from an unexpected change in landing conditions."

The board recommended that commanders review conditions existing at all fields utilized by operational aircraft to insure that all hazards influencing safe operation be included in the field folders and that a policy be established to fix the touchdown point 100 feet down the runway, when possible.

13. <u>Airdrop Delivery</u>

The increasing demand for aerial delivery, that in many cases could not be accomplished by airlanded missions pointed out the need for other delivery methods such as the Parachute Low Altitude Delivery System (PLADS) and the Low Altitude Parachute Extraction System (LAPES). On 31 October, MACV requested 2 AD to consider the feasibility of employing these delivery systems in Vietnam.[69/] The PLADS system could be considered the "baby" of the 315th Air Division, having been developed by a team from the 815th Troop Carrier Squadron in 1963.[70/] However, as of November 1965, only four crews per C-130 squadron were maintaining a PLADS capability and the system had not been proved in combat. The only crews qualified in LAPES and Ground Proximity Extraction System (GPES) delivery methods were those of the TAC rote squadrons.[71/] On 9 December, a message from Hq USAF indicated that at that time the final qualification of the PLADS delivery system was underway in joint tests with the Army at Fort Bragg, N.C. A series of tests for the LAPES system was to begin in January 1966, or as soon as a special type of delivery platform became available.[72/]

Illustrative of the range of assault airlift operations and the efforts required to insure success were the dependent evacuation, early in the year and the strategic airlift against the VC monsoon offensive of mid-1965.

14. Special Missions

Due to increased VC terrorist activities against American forces in Vietnam, highlighted by the night attacks of 7 February in the Pleiku, Tuy Hoa and Nha Trang areas, the forces of the U.S. and RVN combined to launch the first offensive air strikes against NVN territory, hitting the Dong Hoi staging area. This escalation of the conflict led the United States to order, as a protective measure, the evacuation of all U.S. dependents from Vietnam. The 315 AD was called upon to aid in this evacuation and, by 19 February, all of the 1,682 women and children had been evacuated from the country. Letters praising the operation were received from SecDef and CINCPAC.

In August, the Senior Advisor, MACV, II Corps Area, credited the efforts of assault airlift as being instrumental in stemming the tide of the VC offensive in the Central Highlands area. Because of an insufficient number of troops to cover the entire area of action, the Corps Commander relied heavily on strategic airlift to position necessary numbers of troops rapidly, and in key positions, to counter the Viet Cong offensive. In his letter to 2 AD, the Senior Advisor said: 73/

MAJOR AIRLIFTS, 1965

	Dates	Mission	Acft Type	Loads	Pax	Cargo Tons	Flyg Hrs
(1)	TRAINING						
	6-13 Jan	REFLEX I	C-130	120	1,658	1,097	892
	March	LOG TRAIN	C-130	14	293	65	451
	15 Mar-5 May	KITTY 08	C-130	83	264	81	1,350
	14 Apr-16 May	AUMEE IV	C-130	191	461	94	1,067
	4-17 October	PACIFIC CONCORD I	C-130	27	868	214	822
(2)	INTER-THEATER:						
	Jan-July	ABLE MABLE SUPPORT	C-130 / C-124	38 / 11	629	548	696
	7 February	MARINE LAAM BTRY	C-130	52	309	315	836
	4-7 March	GOLDEN WARRIOR	C-130	14	316	100	322
	8-12 March	MARINE CBT LDG TM	C-130	82	1,032	614	920
	4-7 May	ARMY AIRBORNE BRGD	C-130	142	1,878	1,184	1,742
	12-18 May	MARINE CONST BN	C-130 / C-124	46	210	421	600
	19 September	ELDER BLOW	C-130	8	485		?
	6-9 July	1st MARINE AIR WG	C-130	33	342	344	694
(3)	INTRA-THEATER:						
	14 September	ARVN PARADROP	C-130	15	1,125		?
	19-25 October	PLEI ME BATTLE	C-123	29	0	137	?
	25-29 October	1st INFANTRY DIV	C-130	*	11,336	904	?

(*Accomplished by 5 aircraft)

Fig. 8

> "The II Corps Commander, without the truly outstanding tactical airlift provided by the 315th Air Division, would not have been able to hold his own during this critical period. Examples of this airlift include the assembly of six battalions at Hau Bon in early July using a very poor forward airstrip in marginal weather in a 36-hour period; the rapid deployment of a Vietnamese Marine reaction force to Tan Canh in order to retake Dak To District Headquarters in mid-July and subsequently, the assembly of some 14 battalions in order to open Highway 19. In August the 173rd Airborne Brigade was moved, on minimum notice, fron Bien Hoa to Pleiku to provide a reserve force for the successful engagement of the Viet Cong in the Le Thanh District. All these airlifts were performed with an efficiency that demonstrates a high order of professional ability on the part of the aircrews and their supporting echelons...."

The letter was endorsed by MACV, Gen W.C. Westmoreland, and by the Commander 2 AD before it was forwarded to 315 AD.

15. <u>USAF Airlift Evaluation</u>

During the period 11 October-10 November 1965, a special team from Headquarters USAF visited the PACOM area to evaluate airlift operations as they existed in the theater. The conclusions and recommendations of the team are quoted: [74]

> "Part IV: CONCLUSIONS (S)
> A. There are serious deficiencies which severely limit the airlift support capabilities of air terminals in SEA. There is a lack of terminal facilities and a shortage of materials handling equipment as well as spare parts and maintenance "know-how" peculiar to these items of equipment. The aerial port personnel manning posture is unsatisfactory from the standpoint of total number and qualification of assigned personnel. Although some actions are being taken to improve this situation, more immediate action is essential.

B. Within the PACOM area there are presently two airlift systems operating almost independently, as well as two separate priorities and allocations systems. Additionally, operational control of the aerial port squadrons is also divided between the two airlift systems. Fragmentation of these two systems results in inefficient utilization of resources and lack of immediate identification of major problem areas. Present organization and command arrangements are not in consonance with sound management principles.

C. Limited airfield facilities in RVN are constantly saturated by multiple aircraft arrivals. Aircraft flow control is necessary in order to realize optimum advantage of limited ramp space and minimize loss of airframe hours. There is little or no flow control being exercised at the present time into or within SEA.

D. Projected theater airlift movement requirements are not available for more than a month in advance. The fact that approximately 70% of theater airlift capacity is being expended on an on-call basis indicates that the airlift system is reacting primarily to immediate requirements rather than to planned forecasts. The overall system for forecasting intratheater requirements is not accurate on a short range basis and is not designed to provide a longer range projection.

E. The communications necessary for the airlift commander to effectively control his forces are not available for in-country RVN operations and are marginally effective for operations into and out of SEA. If and when known programmed communications improvements materialize, many of the problems associated with control of the airlift force should be alleviated provided that circuits are allocated to the airlift mission on a priority basis.

F. An additional workload is being imposed at air terminal distribution points within SEA by the requirement to repalletize cargo to end destination.

G. MATS channel operations can be established immediately into Da Nang, RVN. The establishment of a channel into Cam Ranh Bay, RVN, can be accomplished now on a restricted basis using C-130 aircraft for primary channel cargo and C-124 aircraft for outsize cargo. The establishment of MATS channels into RVN bases as airlift requirements are identified could assist in alleviating congestion at Tan Son Nhut Air Base.

H. The materiel staff section within the 315th AD should be authorized sufficient manpower to adequately monitor the aircraft maintenance functions of the projected Troop Carrier Wings.

I. As evidenced by review and analysis of pertinent documents and on-the-spot observations, it is apparent that maximum utilization of aircraft ACL's both weight and cube, is not being achieved and that improved utilization is possible.

PART V: RECOMMENDATIONS (S)

A. It is recommended that appropriate Air Staff agencies be directed to:

1. Provide 100% manning in all aerial port units in accordance with grades, AFSC's and skill levels reflected in approved Unit Manning Documents.

2. Develop a study of the air transportation career field to determine actions required to achieve the above objective at the earliest possible date.

3. Insure that airlift terminals are properly located, fully manned and equipped prior to the commencement of extensive airlift operations to preclude a recurrence of the situation now existing at Tan Son Nhut Air Base, RVN.

4. Take aggressive action to insure that programmed communications are operational on a timely basis and required circuitry allocated to the airlift mission as a matter of priority.

5. Establish MATS channels to Cam Ranh Bay and Da Nang at the earliest practicable date.

6. Establish additional MATS channels to SEA when justifiable requirements are known and aircraft turn-around support facilities are available.

7. Request originating terminal operators to completely load individual pallets from the CONUS by end SEA destination whenever feasible.

8. Take the following actions pertaining to the 463L MHE System:

(a) Identify, locate and expedite the movement of equipment to Southeast Asia.

(b) Develop a NORS system comparable to the aircraft NORS system.

(c) Develop an adequate maintenance capability to include technical representation in SEA.

(d) Reevaluate the life expectancy of all equipment.

9. Support PACAF's requirement to augment the materiel staff with 315AD to supervise the maintenance effort of assigned airlift forces.

10. Require PACAF to insure that air terminal procedures provide for the loading of transport aircraft based on the actual, rather than a broad planning ACL.

11. Support the establishment of an Aerial Port Group to act as the central coordinating agency for all PACAF aerial port activities.

12. Deploy Aerial Port packages with deploying airlift forces regardless of whether PCS or TDY status; this will provide a balanced airlift and traffic movement capability.

B. It is recommended that the Chief of Staff, United States Air Force, request the Joint Chiefs of Staff to:

1. Defer deployment of final two PCS C-130E squadrons in Phase I until (a) the effectiveness of MATS route extensions and aerial port and 463L augmentation can be achieved; (b) improved ACL utilization is achieved; and (c) adequate beddown facilities are available. Considering current RVN airfield limitations and overall congestion, if additional airlift capability is deemed essential in the near future it might better be provided by increasing the flying hour utilization rates of the four C-130B model squadrons programmed for PACAF from 2.5 to 3.0 hours and then incrementally to 3.5 hours. The "B" model is particularly adaptable to the SEA mission due to its payload and range characteristics and ease in maintaining. Each .5 hour increase in the PACAF B model force would provide capability equivalent to approximately one additional "B" unit in productive flying hours; i.e., 960 hours per month per each .5 hour increase.

2. Require CINCPAC to establish and implement, without delay, aircraft flow control procedures into and within SEA.

3. Require CINCPAC to institute a system for forecasting more definitive, longer range PACOM intratheater airlift requirements.

4. Require CINCPAC to review PACOM intertheater airlift requirements on a continuing basis to determine the need for establishing additional MATS channels.

5. Require CINCPAC to centralize all Air Force theater airlift resources under the operational control of the 315AD with an operational headquarters at Tan Son Nhut or otherwise appropriately to exercise effective command and control of all airlift resources in SEA.

6. Require CINCPAC to operate a single PACOM priorities and allocations agency in the Pacific Command as outlined in CINCPAC Directive 4600.4a. Implementation of these two single manager concepts (par. 5, above) would result in:

  a. Reduction in the duplication of route structure.
  b. Selective application of the most efficient airframe to mission requirements.
  c. Improved utilization of available ACL's.
  d. Additional overall airlift capability.
  e. More rapid identification and resolution of problem areas.
  f. Greater flexibility to meet other theater contingencies."

16. Summary of Airlift Operations

As of 29 December, in a message to CINCPACAF, the 315AD indicated that C-130 operations in the RVN included 21 C-130 aircraft being utilized on in-country airlift. Two additional C-130's were at Tan Son Nhut for refueling operations and three were at Da Nang for flare support and leaflet drops. The locations of the airlift aircraft were: 11 C-130's at Tan Son Nhut, five at Vung Tau, three at Bien Hoa and four at Nha Trang. [75/]

By the end of December, 1965, the number of passengers and amount of cargo carried with the SEAAS, per month, had risen to 88,067 passengers and 31,708 short tons of cargo. [76]

The C-123 accomplishments for the year were as follows:

	Sorties Flown	Pax Carried	Cargo Airlifted
Jan....	3829	28,140	7436
Feb....	3430	28,222	6248
Mar....	4290	31,109	8023
Apr....	4332	34,926	8248
May....	4271	42,345	9225
Jun....	5574	44,337	9341
Jul....	6348	49,839	11,633
Aug....	6714	49,891	13,255
Sep....	6135	40,228	11,851
Oct....	5622	42,330	9,065
Nov....	5418	42,991	10,595
Dec....	4259	50,174	9,866
Totals..	60,222	484,532	114,786

For total airlift accomplishments refer to Pages 42, 73 and 74. Major airlifts are illustrated on Page 64.

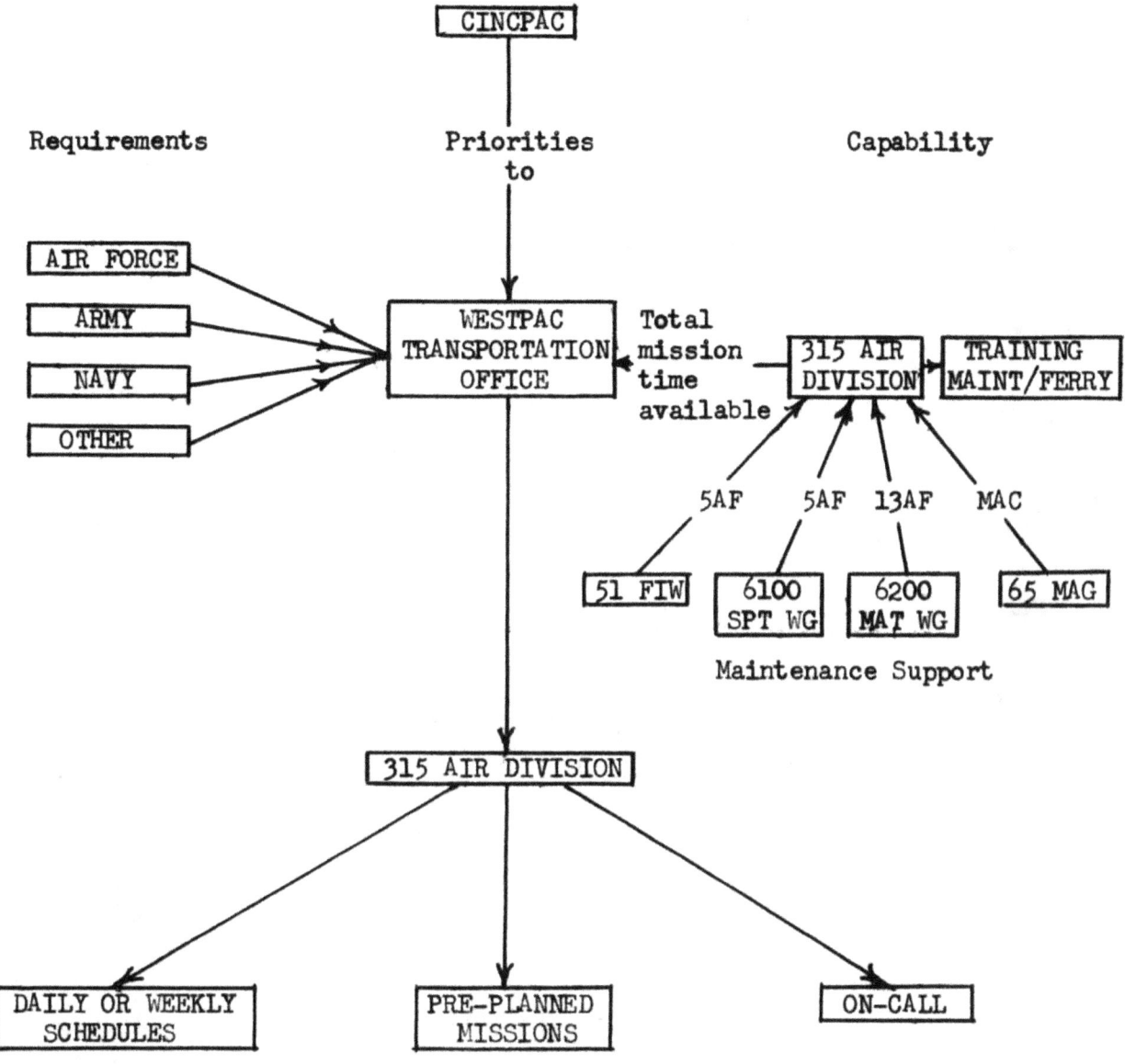

PACIFIC INTRATHEATER AIRLIFT SYSTEM

Fig. 9

PACAF AIRLIFT FORCES

	DC-4	C-118	C-123	C-124	C-130A	C-130B	C-130E
Tachikawa AB							
815 TCS					16		
22 MAS				16			
6485 Ops		4					
Air America	2						
Naha AB							
6315 OPG						64	
Taiwan							
314 TCW							48
Clark AB							
Det 1, 463 TCW					32		
Mactan AB							
463 TCW Hq					32		
Vietnam							
315 ACW			64				
	2	4	64	16	80	64	48

Total Aircraft = 278

Fig. 10

INTRATHEATER AIRLIFT - FLYING HOURS, CY1965

	DC-4 Air America	C-46 Air America	C-54 6485 Ops Sq	C-118 6485 Ops Sq	C-121 MAC	C-124 MAC	C-130 TAC	C-130 315AD	TOTALS
Jan	283	204	159	152	228	1035	1477	2858	6396
Feb	231	223	130	157	226	953	1531	3078	6529
Mar	341	239	222	229	268	1265	1818	3790	8172
Apr	428	198	184	180	229	1260	3825	3887	10191
May	441	217	192	149	294	1151	4329	4387	11160
Jun	462	248	83	291	310	1376	3953	3516	10239
Jul	434	193		340	276	1303	4797	4007	11350
Aug	299	310		351	276	1283	4684	4057	11260
Sep	131	493		362	297	1237	5928	4243	12691
Oct	523			443	310	1255	7065	4171	13767
Nov	514			412	254	1212	7030	4502	13924
Dec	519			334	324	1289	1354	12132	15952
TOTAL	4606	2325	970	3400	3292	14619	47791	54628	131631

Fig 11

AIRLIFT ACCOMPLISHMENTS

Month (1965)	C-123 Aircraft Hit By Ground Fire (No. of Acft.)	Special Forces Support (Tonnage)	Flare Activity (Flares Dropped)	Defoliation Missions (Gals. Dropped)	Tactical Aeromedical Evacuation (No. of Patients)	Intratheater Aeromedical Evacuation in SEA. (No. of Patients)
January	13	2,389	4,371	78,050	9	241
February	15	1,861	5,482	43,000	14	373
March	8	1,705	3,765	28,200	87	384
April	7	1,676	1,549	28,100	93	388
May	15	1,638	3,237	71,600	384	623
June	7	1,352	8,099	0	457	814
July	12	1,330	9,905	31,550	288	1,032
August	21	1,464	5,986	26,700	398	1,470
September	29	2,230	7,344	21,250	375	1,610
October	38	2,194	12,155	81,550	1,406	2,307
November	58	2,683	12,108	119,050	506	3,250
December	49	2,230	6,896	158,500	507	2,285
TOTALS	272 Hits	22,752 Tons	80,897 Flares	687,550 Gallons	4,524 Patients	14,777 Patients (SEA)

Fig. 12

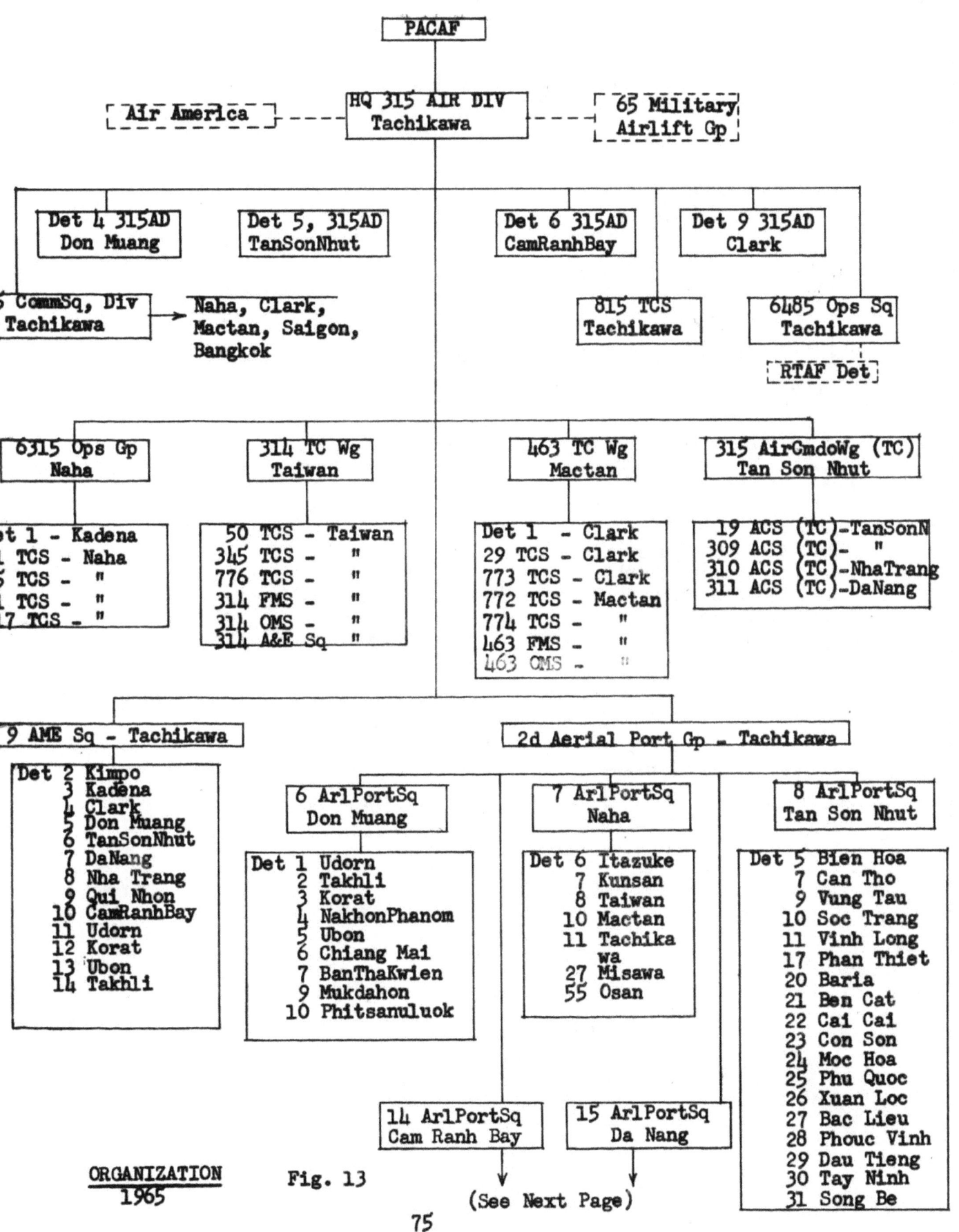

ORGANIZATION 1965   Fig. 13

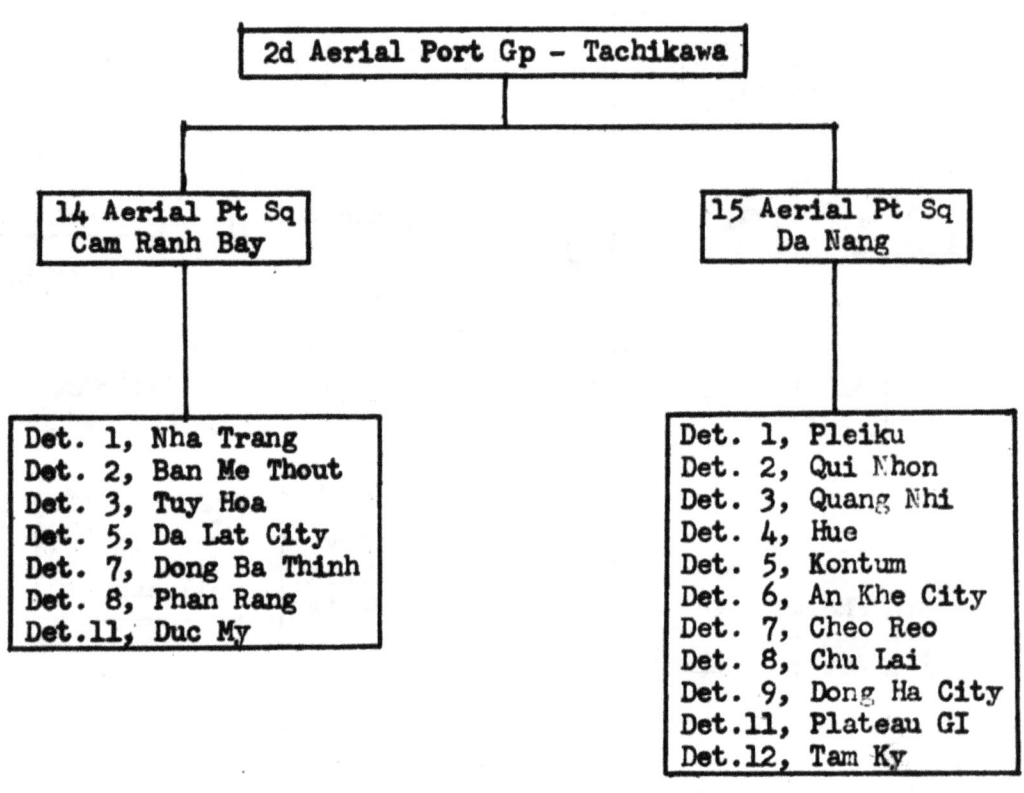

Fig. 13
(Continued from Preceding Page)

CHAPTER VII - 1966.

1. <u>Organizational Structure</u>

The Southeast Asia organizational structure, as applied to airlift, is shown below:

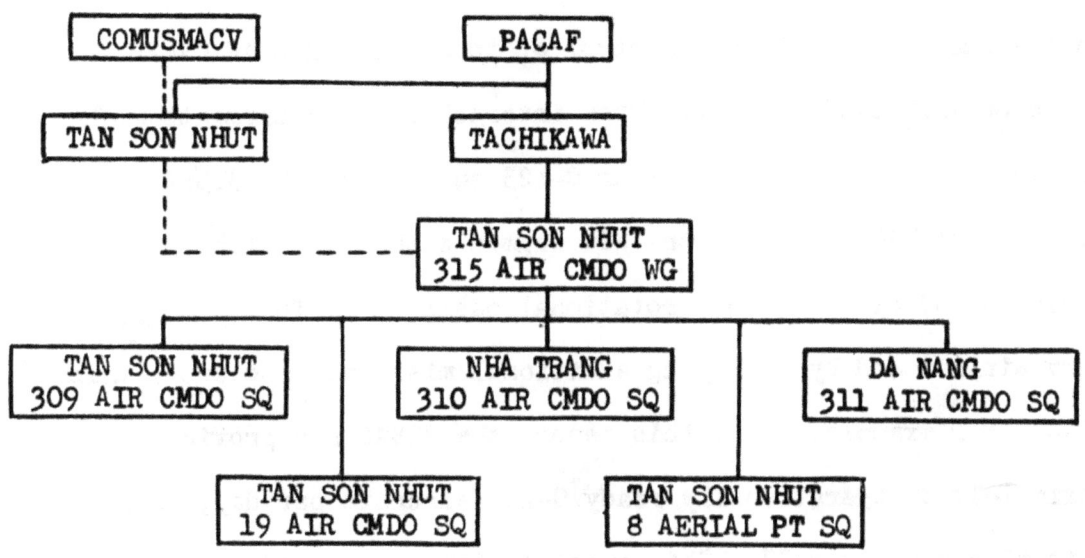

Fig. 14

Noteworthy is the fact that MACV is not assigned command of any Air Force airlift forces. The 7AF, physically located in-country, is under the operational control of COMUSMACV and command control of PACAF. The Commander, 7AF, is the Air Force component commander for COMUSMACV. The 315th Air Commando Wing, also at Tan Son Nhut, is under the operational control of 7AF and command control of 315AD, Tachikawa AB, Japan. The 7AF and 315AD are at the same command level in the PACAF organizational structure.

The 315AD supports requirements generated in Japan, Korea, Okinawa, Taiwan and the Philippines, in addition to supporting a second airlift force known as the Southeast Asia Airlift System (SEAAS).

The SEAAS supports airlift requirements exclusively within the RVN and Thailand. The 315th ACW operates the SEAAS. To perform this mission, the 315th ACW is assigned four C-123 Air Commando Squadrons and has operational control of three to six RAAF CV-2B (Caribou or Wallaby) aircraft. When internal RVN requirements exceed the capabilities of the four C-123 squadrons, the 315AD, at the request of MACV, through the WTO augments the 315th ACW by providing C-130 aircraft on a rotational basis to perform in-country airlift and by operating additional missions into and within the RVN. For example, as of this report the 315AD has provided approximately 30 operationally ready C-130 aircraft per day, on a rotational basis, to MACV. This augmentation has surged temporarily to as many as 60 C-130 O/R aircraft. It is planned to increase the RVN C-130 rotational force to approximately 58 O/R aircraft by December, 1966, to meet MACV forecast in-country airlift requirements. No formal arrangement exists for operational control of the rotational force in the RVN to pass from 315AD to 7AF, but in actuality this does occur. The C-130 rotational force responds to MACV requirements from frag orders which are published by the 315th ACW.

2. Command and Control

The present command and control system has two agencies which establish priorities and allocations to which the intra-theater airlift force must respond, these are the Western Transportation Office (WTO) and the Traffic Management Agency (TMA).

The Western Transportation Office (WTO) is collocated with the 315AD at Tachikawa AB, Japan, and is a part of J4 CINCPAC. The WTO is charged with insuring optimum utilization of air and sealift resources for the support of PACOM forces in the WESTPAC. In October 1965, the buildup of U.S. forces in Vietnam resulted in the establishment of a joint airlift/sealift branch office in Saigon. This office also has the responsibility for Thailand and is designated WTO-B. In the near future, a branch office is scheduled to open at Don Muang AB, Pangkok, Thailand.

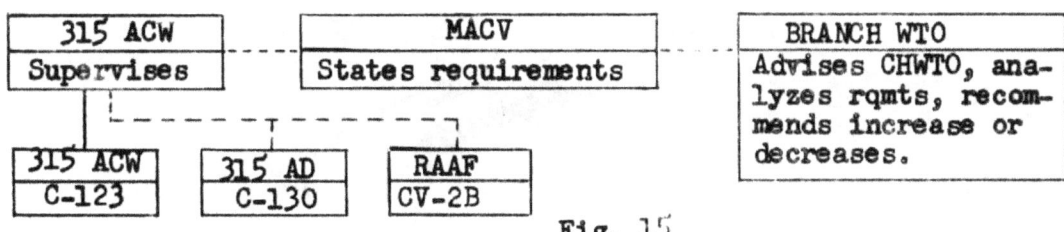

Fig. 15

With Vietnam, MACV has established a Traffic Management Agency (TMA), under the staff supervision of the J4 MACV. The TMA reviews the total transportation requiremnts is the RVN, allocates available ground, sea and airlift capability and directs traffic based on priority, to the various modes of delivery. In addition, MACV has established a Joint Movements Transportation Board (JMTB) for allocation of space on all common service transportation for scheduled movement of personnel and materiel in the MACV area of responsibility. The JMTB meets monthly or more often, if necessary.

The functions of the WTO and TMA are essentially the same. Although there is no evidence that these command and control arrangements have adversely affected the airlift mission, a delay factor must be an inherent part of such a system. For example, when in-country RVN airlift requirements exceed the capabilities of the 315th Air Commando Wing, TMA in Saigon must request additional airlift capability from the WTO located at Tachikawa AB, Japan. Upon review and approval by the WTO, the additional airlift capability is provided by 315AD.

The operation of the Airlift Request Net in SEA is shown below:

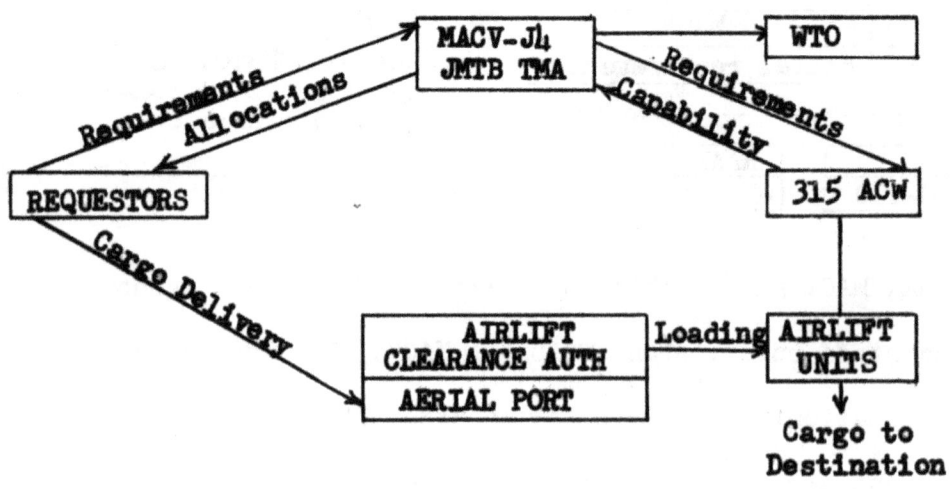

Fig. 16

CHTWO is a CINCPAC staff function "... to insure the optimum utilization of airlift and sealift resources provided by the 315 AD and COMSTSFE, for tactical, training and logistical support of PACOM forces in the WESTPAC area..." This mission and the resources are separate form Military Airlift Command (MAC). The intra-theater airlift supplements the MAC airlift, and the only time WTO will perform airlift over MAC channel routes is when the request for airlift indicated that such MAC airlift is not available, or the required delivery date (RDD) cannot be met by use of MAC. 77/

In July 1966, CINCPAC was proposing to abolish CHWTO and replace it with a Joint Transportation Board at CINCPAC. 78/

3. Requests, Allocations & Priorities

When a request for airlift is received by WTOB, it is reviewed by the requesting service's representative for accuracy and completeness and is then evaluated somewhat on the "who, why, where, when" philosophy.

Use of the CINCPAC mission priority system and urgency of movement (RDD) are two essentials for evaluation. The mission priorities are:

    1 - General war plans.
    2 - Emergency deployment of PACOM forces.
    3 - Support of forces on emergency deployment.
    4 -- Medical evacuation.
    5 - CINCPAC-directed missions.

6 - Training.
7 - Normal support of forces not on emergency deployment.
8 - TDY, emergency leave.
9 - All others.

Priorities 2 and 3 are most frequently used in unit troop movements, deployments and logistical ("follow-on") support. [79]

COMUSMACV further expands these priorities for operations in Southeast Asia: [80]

1 - TAC emergency (tactical movement into combat).
2 - Emergency resupply (supply of primary materials essential to forces in combat).
3 - Combat essential (unplanned movements of units or supplies for which an operational requirement exists which justifies the disruption of planned transportation).

   a. Units, weapons and supplies essential to operational mission.

   b. Auxiliary equipment, lack of which would impair operation.

   c. Administrative troop movement; essential supply for administrative support; emergency repair of administrative equipment; other than routine supply.

   c. Routine resupply.

   d. Training.

A forecast of non-tactical and tactical requirements is established by COMUSMACV for the calendar year. A monthly allocation of flying hours is given the WTO to meet the requirements of the services. More often than not, these requirements exceed the flying hours available. The latter are apportioned in three general categories:

      a. Daily or weekly schedules.
      b. Pre-planned missions.
      c. On-call missions.

On-call missions are the day-to-day "special project" requests for immediate needs which cannot be forecasted. They are usually "short notice" and "immediate response" in nature. This category will, in some cases, require a delay or cancellation of either the scheduled or pre-planned missions. It then becomes the WTO's responsibility to follow CINCPAC procedures for utilizing C-130 aircraft as follows: 81/

      a. Supplemental (shuttle) Aircraft: In considering airlift requirements, CHWTO determines the amount of C-130 capability and, based on priorities, makes the necessary allocations.

      b. Operational Control (In-Country): 315AD shuttle aircraft are under the operational control of the Airlift Command designated by 7AF (315th Air Commando Wing) upon arrival at an RVN staging base and reverts to 315AD operational control upon departure for out-country destinations.

      c. Operational Control (Other): Operational control remains with 315AD on all 315AD aircraft transiting RVN bases on schedules or special missions. Requests for diversion of these flights are addressed to WTOB, RVN, info CHWTO, and subsequent diversion authority is issued by the 315AD Commander, as required.

The WTOB provides the local SEA contact with MACV J-4, MACV TMA, 7AF Airlift Command representatives (including the ALCC),

Det. 5-315AD, and senior RVN representatives.

To ensure understanding of a complicated request, allocation and priority system, a brief review of the functions of the various agencies involved follows:

MACV J-4 receives airlift requests. Based on these requests, the Joint Movement Transportation Board (JMTB) allocates airlift on a monthly bases. The Traffic Management Agency (TMA), also a part of MACV J-4, reviews priorities and processes the requests to the Airlift Control Center (ALCC). The ALCC functions as the principal scheduling point for all transport aircraft under the operational control of the 7AF in South Vietnam. When the ALCC receives the airlift requirements from MACV J-4, they select the type of aircraft movement best suited to meet the specific airlift destination airfield, cargo size, etc. The ALCC and subordinate Transport Movement Control (TMC) effects the necessary coordination with Wing commanders, separate squadron commanders, detachment commanders and the WTOB, as required, to insure optimum use of available resources.

4. <u>Command Post & Scheduling Branch</u>

The overall operation is carried out by the ALCC's Command Post and Scheduling Branch. The command post operates on a 24-hour day, 7-day week schedule, and maintains visual flight-following boards and a permanent log of aircraft movements for aircraft under operational control of the 315th Air Commando Wing in SEA, and 315th Air Division aircraft operating throughout the RVN. Status boards reflect current weather, aircraft status, location of key personnel and combat control teams. The command post also initiates, coordinates and monitors maintenance and security support for aircraft out of commission at isolated stations and initiates SAR (search and rescue) for overdue aircraft. Diversions of aircraft to tactical emergency missions (TAC-E), or direct assignment to this type of mission, are accomplished by the CP.

Aeromedical evacuations (medevac) in-country (on an emergency basis) are fulfilled by diverting an aircraft into the required area. Routine medevac flights out-country are handled by aircraft returning from the in-country shuttle. Scheduled or special project flights are used extensively for this purpose.

The scheduling section publishes and distributes a monthly schedule of pre-planned missions and daily frag orders directing special missions. This section also determines the requirements for mission commanders, combat control teams (CCT) and aerial port mobility teams, and directs their deployment as required. If it is determined that fighter escort is required for a particular mission, the scheduling section initiates action to obtain the necessary air cover. Security and suitability of airfields and landing/drop zones (LZ/DZ) are ascertained prior to airlift operations. Daily scheduling meetings are held with the flying organizations

to coordinate and set up the following day's flying schedule.
Joint service mission planning meetings, obtaining diplomatic
clearances and maintaining a current ready-reference list of
operational airfields are some of the additional responsibilities
of the scheduling section of the ALCC.

The director of the ALCC is also responsible for the supervision
of the subordinate transport movement control units (TMC's). These
act as an extension of the ALCC. At present there are seven TMC's
located in the RVN, with an additional five programmed. Operational
TMC's are located at Tan Son Nhut, Nha Trang, Da Nang, Cam Ranh Bay,
Pleiku, Oui Nhon and Bien Hoa. Scheduled for activation are TMC's
at Ban Me Thout, Ben Thuy, An Khe, Hue, and Vung Tau.

The TMC provides service for tactical airlift units by
coordinating and monitoring all phases of airlift. This includes
liaison with shippers and aerial port facilities to insure expeditious and timely movement of troops and cargo on scheduled and
non-scheduled airlift missions. Maintenance and refueling operations
are monitored and coordinated to expedite mission accomplishment.

As directed by the WTO, 315AD responsibility is to: Position
sufficient operational airframes and trained aircrews in the RVN
and Thailand to accomplish airlift mission requirement; to establish
equitable aircrew/aircraft rotational policies; insure proper
aircrew training, standardization and qualification to perform

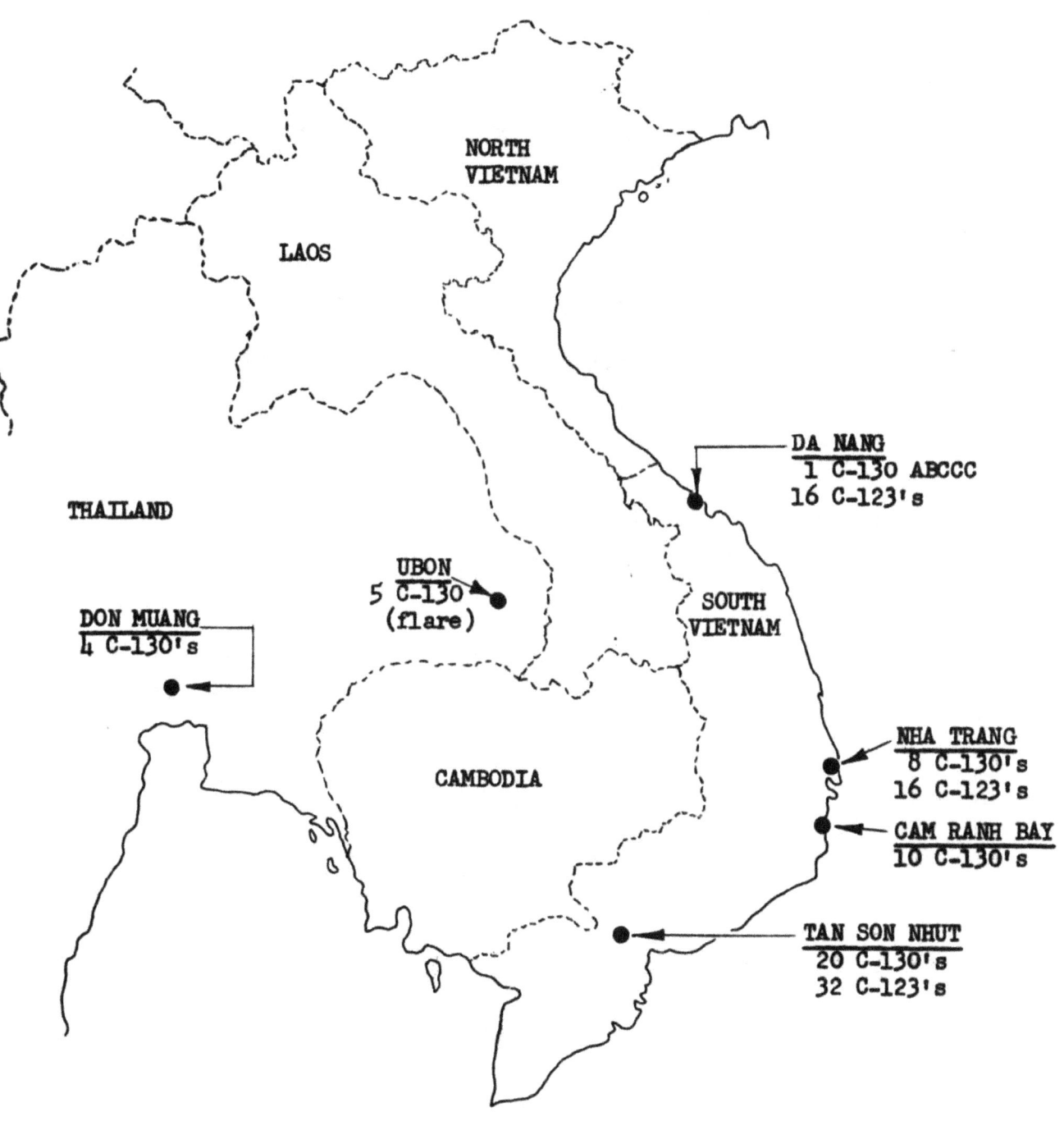

SEA AIRLIFT AIRCRAFT LOCATIONS
(AS of 30 June 1966)

Fig. 17

SOUTHEAST ASIA FORCE STRENGTH vs. AIRLIFT ACTIVITY

Month (1966)	Personnel in SEA	Tonnage Airlifted Within RVN	PAX Airlifted Within RVN
Jan	216,988	39,360	95,772
Feb	230,484	33,694	87,328
Mar	255,640	44,363	102,479
Apr	273,670	45,495	109,020
May	284,606	45,505	110,457
Jun	297,677	49,500	124,923
Jul	312,376	50,159	131,027
		308,076	761,006

Sources: Personnel - USAF Mgt, Summary SEA, & SEA Stat Reporting OASD (Compt) Tonnage - 315AD Report, 8 Feb 66, & Opnl Acty Rpt (OPSACT), C-123, CV-2, (RAAF) and C-130 acty only.

Fig. 18

mission assignments; delegate authority, as required, to detachments and mission commanders to accomplish airlift missions timely and effectively.

Aircraft requirements which cannot be met by C-130 aircraft staged in Thailand and under the scheduling/traffic control of Det 4 of the 6th Aerial Port Squadron (Don Muang AF, Thailand) are forwarded to WTOB RVN/THAI, Tan Son Nhut AB, with information copies to CHWTO.

5. Problem Areas

Despite the USAF Special Evaluation Team visit to PACOM during the latter part of 1965, with their attendant conclusions and recommendations, many of the problems continued to plague airlift operations. Of these problems, the following continued to be of major concern:

    a. Centralized Control:

The Commander, 7AF is faced with a lack of centralized control in that he commands only a limited amount of the airlift forces operating in his area of responsibility. The C-130 fleet and the aerial port units are assigned to units in other commands. On 3 May 1966, General Moore, Commander 7AF, proposed that the in-country airlift structure be reorganized to include a troop carrier division assigned directly to 7 AF. The air division would be composed of a wing of C-123's, a C-130 wing, a CV-2 wing and an aerial port group. CINCPACAG indicated agreement with the proposal excepting the C-130 wing. It was felt the TDY concept of C-130 operations should be retained. It was proposed that a TAC airlift airdivision be deployed to the RVN not later than 1 July 1966, and that a CV-2 wing headquarters be formed by 1 September. 83/ Headquarters 315AD concurred with PACAF. 84/ The CSAF, in his answer to CINC PACAF, concurred with PACAF's proposal and suggested that, after activation of the air division, consideration be given to inactivation of the air divsiion (315th AD) and the transfer of theater airlift to 7AF. 85/ TAC also concurred and indicated designation of the air division would follow USAF approval of the division's deployment. 86/ The air division is scheduled for activation in September, and the 2d Aerial Port Group, presently located at Tachikawa AB, Japan, is scheduled to deploy to Tan Son Nhut AB, South Vietnam, in December. MACV, following a briefing by 7AF in July, agreed with the concept of the air division and its deployment to the RVN.

    b. Forward Operating Bases:

    The strategic airlift force, MAC, presently terminates channel traffic at only three bases in the RVN - Cam Ranh Bay, Da Nang, and Saigon. On special airlift assignments, however, MAC operates into other fields in the RVN, i.e., the special airlift of the 25th Army Division from Hawaii to Pleiku. This results in double handling of inbound cargo. (Once upon theater arrival (off-load) and again into the SEA system (on-load). It is handled again at its destination airfield, either by another aerial port unit or, in some instances, by the users.

    c. Parking and Loading/Unloading Areas:

    All of the air bases are congested and sufficient ramp space is not available to efficiently operate the aerial port system. Many bases are so congested that aircraft have to be backed in and out of parking spaces - an unsafe practice which also places additional strain on landing gear already over-stressed by assault landings and takeoffs on substandard airfields. Many of the smaller airfields are so insecure that aircraft cannot RON because of the danger of attack by enemy forces using mortars, recoilless rifles - even the use of satchel charges by infiltrators.

    d. Communications:

    The ALCC has, at the present time, only land-line communications with its subordinate TMC's, and only two of these are "hot lines." The remainder have to be called through the regular long-distance switchboards, usually a frustrating and unproductive effort. Communications are practically non-existent between the ALCC and the aerial port or combat control units in the field. Communication with airborne aircraft, necessary in the event of inflight diversion or advisory, is very unreliable. Programmed communication systems, when installed and operational, will greatly facilitate the command and control vital to the widespread SEA tactical situation. Programmed equipment includes: 87/

   (1) UHF ground stations to enable TMC's to communicate with all agencies and aircraft to facilitate offload/onload and turn-around of aircraft. (Programmed operational in March 1967.)

   (2) An HF, single sideband, air-to-ground, point-to-point communication system to provide communications for control of SEA airlift operations. (Estimated operational by October 1966.)

   (3) A teletype circuit to support airlift missions is being installed between the ALCC at Tan Son Nhut and TMC's in the RVN. This system will be secure and will have a capacity for 100 words per minute and should fulfill airlift teletype requirements. (Estimated completion date FY 2/67.)

Until the communications systems are operational, it is difficult, if not impossible, for controlling agencies to notify destination airfields and users of a diversion, cancellation or delay in flights. Many users feel the airlift request net is too cumbersome, unwieldy and unresponsive for TAC emergency airlift requests. The question of using the Tactical Control System (TACS) communications for forwarding requests in the manner of requesting fighter strikes, is often raised. At times, the only timely airlift request information is secured when the USAF Airlift Liaison Officer (ALO) and the requesting Army unit informally notifies them of the incoming request.

   e. Personnel and Material Handling Equipment:

Overseas requirements for Air Transportation Supervisors (AFSC 60770) exceeds the CONUS resources. As a result, personnel are assigned from other career fields. Training in SEA is not feasible due to workloads and the short, 12-month tour of duty. In April 1966, the 8th Aerial Port Squadron (Tan Son Nhut AB) had only 166 personnel assigned against an authorized strength of 314. Material handling equipment was in very short supply and that which was in the theater had an excessive out-of-commission rate for maintenance and spare parts. On 30 November 1965, the MHE in-commission rate was only 60 percent.

f. Orientation, Familiarization and Knowledge of Airlift Systems:

Many times aircraft have been requested only to have ground delays upon arrival at the pickup point because the Army did not have the loads properly rigged or palletized. Other instances occur when loads have been prepared for C-130 lift only to have C-123's arrive to furnish the airlift.

g. Crew Manning:

While the C-123's are assigned into the RVN on a PCS basis, the C-130's stage into the country in TDY status. The majority of the main operating bases from which the C-130's operate are in a longer tour area (18 months or longer) than is the case in SEA. As a result, many crew members spend the great majority of their time in SEA on TDY but, as of now, do not get credit for the SEA tour. With the critical shortage of C-130 qualified aircrews throughout the USAF, many of the crews feel that upon their return to the ZI, since they do not receive credit for the SEA tour, they will be immediately returned to SEA as crew members.

h. Crew Proficiency:

CINCPACAF has had to grant waivers on many of the normal training requirements for crews to remain tactically qualified. The original AF strike crews deployed to PACOM were well qualified. An outstanding job of incorporating training into the regularly scheduled airlift missions has resulted in very little unproductive flying time from the standpoint of cargo and passengers airlifted. The fact remains, however, that three of the last four C-130 accidents in SEA were attributed to pilot error. 88/ With the imminent departure of the original crews, many replacements will be arriving with relatively little C-130 flying time and, in many cases, low amounts of flying time. Unless crew proficiency improves, the accident rate is bound to increase. 89/

i. Aging Aircraft:

The VNAF is equipped with an aging fleet of C-47's. The USAF Advisory Group, Vietnam, has recommended these aircraft be replaced with C-119G's. To better prepare the VNAF for its continuing role in the future airlift operation, it is imperative a modernization program be implemented to further augment the SEA airlift system. 90/

j. Aircraft Configuration:

The C-130 was not specifically designed for the assault role. Of necessity, however, it has been so committed. The inability of this aircraft to adequately perform the assault airlift mission under other than VFR conditions is well known. Even though the C-130 airlift fleet is aging, it will be the backbone of the fleet for the foreseeable future. Until C-130J and/or V-STOL aircraft are procured, the all-weather delivery capability of the C-130 fleet needs to be improved, particularly in station-keeping capability and in radar and computer navigation. 91/

k. Diversion of Aircraft:

Requirements for defoliation and flare missions and airborne command post flights, diverts many airframes from the assault airlift system. Until new aircraft types are developed or modified to take over these functions, the C-123 spray aircraft, plus the C-130 flare and airborne command post aircraft, will be unavailable to help meet the increasing requirements for assault airlift. 92/

l. Reporting Procedures:

Prior to July 1966, there has been a definite lack of reporting procedures and channels to adequately document the complete SEA airlift system (SEAAS). There was no one, single source of information which could be used to document the total amount of airlift support which went into a typical tactical support mission. Special airlift cargo was placed on scheduled mission flights and no adequate identification of the nature of this cargo and/or passengers was available to researchers for documentation. The automated Airlift Reporting System (scheduled for implementation in July 1966, but not yet operational) was designed in response to an urgent, continuing requirement for detailed data relating to airlift operations in the PACOM area, particularly in SEA. The reports will deal with aircraft operations, mission performance, traffic (passengers and cargo) movement and aerial port cargo handling. This reporting system will be operated through the Command Control System and is designed to accept data inputs from Air Terminal and Air Operations sources.

6. Projected Requirements

By the end of December, 1965, the number of passengers and amount of cargo carried within the SEAAS per month had risen to 88,067 passengers and 31,708 short tons of cargo. During April 1966, the passenger airlift rose to 109,020 and cargo lift increased to 45,495 short tons. 93/ (See Page 88.)

In a typical month, airlift account for 31 percent of the total weight transported by U.S. carriers in the RVN. The remainder moved by rail (4%), water (37%) and truck (28%).

In its analysis of C-130 operations in-country, for June 1966, the 315th ACW reported that each C-130 was carrying 33.8 tons per day for a total airlift of 40,577 tons for the month. 94/

As representative of operations in the RVN, the 315th ACW ALCC reported that, for June 1966, 48 tactical emergency missions, 130 emergency resupply missions and 13 combat-essential missions were levied by MACV J-4. An additional 550 routine requests for special airlift were received. 95/

In June 1966, the breakdown of the total airlift force available for the SEA Airlift System was:

```
C-130A.................. 80
C-130B.................. 64
C-130E.................. 48
C-123................... 64
```

Of this total available force, 38 C-130's were staged in the RVN, four in Thailand, with the C-123's permanently stationed in the RVN. 96/ (See Page 87.)

ASSAULT AIRLIFT IN SUPPORT OF GROUND OPERATIONS
(Jan-Sep 1966)

Sources: PACAF RCS AF-J38 & Airlift Reports

DATES 1966	MISSION	No. of Sorties C-123	No. of Sorties C-130	PAX	CARGO (Tons)
25 Jan-27 Jan	MASHER	32		1268	9
25 Feb-27 Feb	GARFIELD		168	2041	1720
10 Mar-30 Apr	MOONLIGHT	13	68	5515	*
25 Mar-31 Mar	LINCOLN		36	970	208
30 Mar	ABILENE		42	1252	187
8 Apr-14 Apr	AUSTIN V		228	3640	2363
10 Apr-13 Apr	DENVER	10	138	1237	1529
15 Apr	LONGFELLOW		26	850	136
16 Apr-17 Apr	MOSBY I		36	1592	230
20 Apr-24 Apr	GEORGIA	135		1256	685
21 Apr- 4 May	MOSBY II		61	1879	423
24 Apr-16 May	BIRMINGHAM	208	459	5591	6822
26 Apr-14 May	AUSTIN VI	19	302	2573	3135
19 May-26 May	COOPER		198	2564	1862
26 May	EL PASO I		19	291	168
29 May- 3 Jun	HAWTHORNE		204	1662	2046
? May**	VIRGINIA	206		1256	286
2 Jun-13 Jul	EL PASO II	2438	837	14742	9097
16 Jun-21 Jul	BEAUREGARD		361	1829	2198
20 Jun	DECKHOUSE		77	658	275
24 Jun- 5 Jul	NATHAN HALE		105	1019	246
2 Jul-31 Jul	HENRY CLAY		346	3363	1465
3 Jul-31 Jul	KAHAMA	57	24	491	152
9 Jul-17 Jul	AURORA	153	106	807	1183
13 Jul- 3 Sep	EL PASO III	2586	819	15985	10458
15 Jul- 5 Sep	JOHN PAUL JONES		316	2885	2622
14 Aug-31 Aug	PAUL REVERE	94	321	2003	1432
24 Aug-23 Sep	POLESTAR		254	2232	1389
26 Aug-(Cont'g)	BYRD		188	783	1074

* Troop Baggage Only
** Airlift of U.S. Marines

Fig. 19

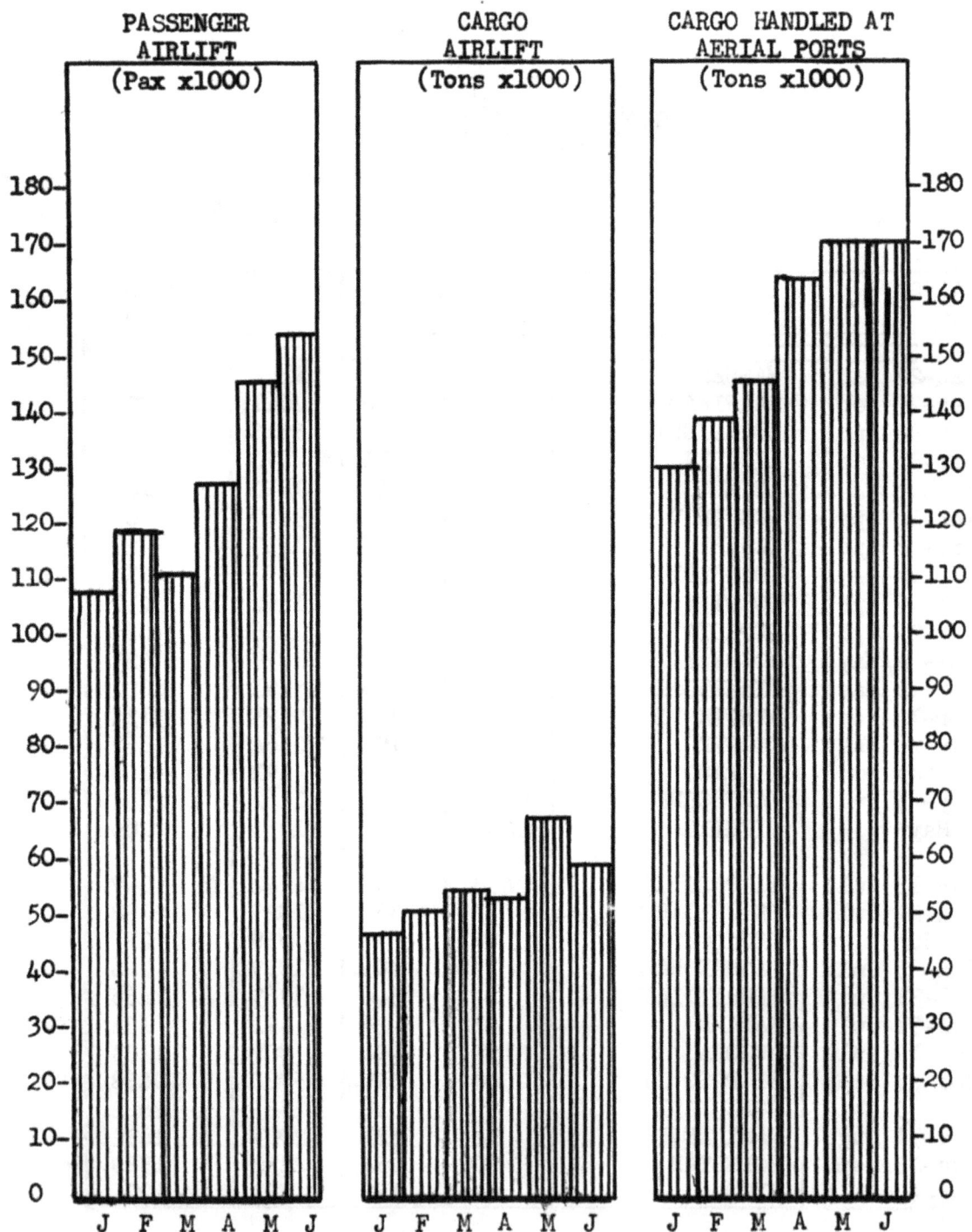

TOTAL SEAAS PASSENGER & CARGO AIRLIFT
(First Half CY 1966)

Fig. 20

Projected requirements for C-130 airframes by the end of the 1966 calendar year were: [97/]

    RVN Shuttle.................. 58
    Other Intra-Theater 79
    Alert Pad 7
    Flare Missions 6
    Training 10

      Total 160

Although the airlift accomplishment increased sharply, it did not catch up with the monthly forecast of requirements which was prepared by MACV. In January 1966 the actual lift equaled 73% of the forecast and, in June, 74%. In July, MACV revised its forecast downward by about 15% for the remainder of FY 1966. The July airlift amounted to 84% of the revised forecast.

The available data indicate that the current airlift operation is moving cargo at such a rate that aerial port inventories are kept below planned levels, and that air shipment of cargo has reportedly been adequate in its support of forces in the theater. Examination of the daily transportation reports indicated that the available aircraft are moving the current aerial port cargo in sufficient volume. [98/]

7. **C-123 Activity**

The 64 C-123 aircraft are based at three locations in the RVN: Tan Son Nhut(32), Nha Trang(16) and Da Nang(16). The flying time expended per possessed aircraft has gradually increased since January 1965 from 2.2 hours per day to 3.4 in July 1966. (See Page 99.)

97

During June 1966, a total of 5763 flying hours were logged, of which
1.9 percent (1112 hours) was applied against other than logistics
missions (i.e. flare and defoliation).

8. CV-2 Activity

The RAAF CV-2 aircraft are located at Vung Tau and fly in
support of the requirements identified by the 315th ACW. Missions
such as the support of Special Forces camps and U.S. AID are examples
in which small tonnages and numbers of passengers are required and
the use of the CV-2 capability is most productive. During 1965, the
six CV-2 aircraft averaged a 2.4-hour daily utilization rate, while
in 1966 the average rose to 2.8 hours per day. The total tonnage
(cargo and passenger) carried by the CV-2's is quite stable,
slightly more than 1,000 short tons per month. (See Page 100.)

9. Army CV-2 Activity

The U.S. Army CV-2 aircraft are assigned throughout the RVN at
nine locations, as of 31 July 1966: Da Nang (4), Pleiku (20), Qui
Nhon (7), Nha Trang (5), Dong Ba Thin (14), Tan Son Nhut (2), Vung
Tau (33), Can Tho (8) and Soc Trang (5), for a total of 98 aircraft.
These aircraft operate in direct support of Army units and are
responsive to the corps or division commander's needs. Each of
six aviation companies has assigned 16 aircraft and 40 pilots. The
pilots average 72 hours per month and may fly no more than 120 hours.
Since January 1966, the daily utilization rate for the possessed
aircraft has averaged 2.4 hours per day, or slightly less than the

C-123 DETAILED AIRLIFT ACTIVITY
(Source: 315AD/ACW Records)

Month (1965)	Sorties	Flying Time	Avg Pos	S/T Cargo	Pax	Total S/T Pax & Cargo	Avg Daily Util Rate Pos Acft
Jan	3960	4292	63	7,398	28,042	10,202	2.2
Feb	3630	4089	63	6,747	28,219	9,569	2.3
Mar	4304	4572	64	8,376	31,054	11,481	2.3
Apr	4580	4676	60	8,545	35,909	12,136	2.6
May	5312	5148	58	9,056	42,346	13,290	2.9
Jun	5447	5383	58	9,923	46,506	14,662	3.1
Jul	6016	5802	56	10,943	50,307	16,046	3.3
Aug	6528	6448	63	12,373	49,130	17,286	3.3
Sep	6439	6495	63	12,509	48,657	17,376	3.4
Oct	6088	6130	62	11,768	50,375	16,805	3.3
Nov	6312	5606	62	12,455	49,304	17,385	3.0
Dec	5823	4959	58	10,757	45,875	15,344	2.8
(1966) Jan	6670	5265	56	12,549	46,382	18,113	3.0
Feb	5727	4899	56	10,659	37,646	15,834	3.1
Mar	6856	5285	51	13,751	47,420	19,441	3.3
Apr	6911	5229	49	12,975	41,103	17,907	3.6
May	7246	5666	49	13,761	45,388	19,207	3.7
Jun	8066	5763	52	15,425	49,243	21,334	3.7
Jul	8460	5811	55	16,489	52,449	22,782	3.4

Fig. 21

RAAF CV-2 ACTIVITY

Month (1965)	Sorties	Flying Time	Avg Pos	S/T Cargo	Pax	Total S/T Pax & Cargo	Avg Daily Util Rate Pos Acft
Jan	837	509	6	724	3,786	1,178	3.28
Feb	824	495	6	680	3,383	1,086	2.75
Mar	737	410	6	772	2,956	1,127	2.28
Apr	688	386	6	626	3,359	1,031	2.14
May	605	380	6	501	2,590	812	2.14
Jun	362	242	6	325	1,533	509	1.34
Jul	752	487	6	586	3,985	1,065	2.71
Aug	589	378	6	502	2,573	811	2.10
Sep	802	481	6	622	4,434	1,154	2.67
Oct	740	466	6	520	4,536	1,064	2.59
Nov	774	463	6	659	4,174	1,160	2.57
Dec	768	493	6	803	4,695	1,366	2.74
(1966) Jan	717	437	6	622	3,804	992	2.43
Feb	759	495	6	702	3,639	1,139	2.75
Mar	890	546	6	767	4,357	1,290	3.03
Apr	880	548	6	698	4,214	1,204	3.04
May	789	546	6	702	3,111	1,075	3.03
Jun	855	480	6	710	3,552	1,136	2.66
Jul	638	*	6	480	2,730	808	*

Note: *=Data not available.   Source: 315AD Records

Fig. 22

ARMY CV-2 ACTIVITY

Month (1966)	Sorties	Flying Time	Avg Pos	S/T Cargo	Pax	Total S/T Pax & Cargo	Avg Daily Util Rate Pos Acft
Jan	6,058	3,767	63	2,421	24,376	5,346	1.99
Feb	9,559	7,028	100	6,379	56,040	13,093	2.34
Mar	11,949	7,066	104	7,537	69,126	15,833	2.26
Apr	12,545	7,776	101	7,802	78,438	17,214	2.57
May	11,170	7,600	101	6,302	69,414	14,631	2.51
Jun	12,689	8,026	99	6,206	58,231	13,193	2.70
Jul	11,638	7,356	99	6,121	58,993	13,200	2.48

Note: Total tonnage represents cargo tons added to pax weight at the rate of .12 tons (240 lbs.) per passenger.

Data for 1965 not available.

Fig. 23

six RAAF CV-2's over the same period. (See Page 101.) The CV-2 aircraft have a 6000-pound planning ACL for a 100nm radius of flight and can operate out of primitive airfields with runways approximately 1200 feet long.

The largest proportion of the airlift in the RVN is in support of U.S. Army forces in-country. A breakdown of C-123 and C-130 activity during the month of June 1966 reveals the following:

> C-123: Sixty-eight percent of the cargo and 58 percent of the passengers were moved in support of U.S. Army forces. Other prime users of the airlift were the VNAF and the U.S. Marine Corps. Considering the types of cargo carried, 43 percent was general cargo, 26 percent fuel, 11 percent food and 20 percent explosives.
>
> C-130: Seventy-seven percent of the cargo and 61 percent of the passengers were moved in support of Army operations, with the USAF, VNAF, U.S. Navy and Marine Corps as secondary users. The distribution of cargo by type carried by the C-130 is similar to the C-123 with 50 percent cargo, 19 percent fuel, 10 percent food and 21 percent explosives.

10. RVN Airfields

There are over 200 air bases in the RVN published for use by the 315th Air Commando Wing. The preponderance of these strips are of various natural surfaces - sod, clay, dirt/earth, and sand. A particular type of soil - "laterite," a reddish iron-rich soil formed by the decomposition of rocks - comprises many of the earth-surfaced runways. Several strips are surfaced with M-8 pierced steel planking (PSP) and M8A1 PSP but without holes; some with aluminum matting (AM-2) of MX19, and a few with T-17 nylon and neoprene membrane. Very few are surfaced with asphalt or concrete. Only 20% of the operational airfields are fully suitable for C-130 use and an additional 16% are considered marginal. Specific restrictions were recently imposed on airfields the C-130A could use. The runways must be 4500' or longer. Suitable C-130 airfields, with their locations, follows:

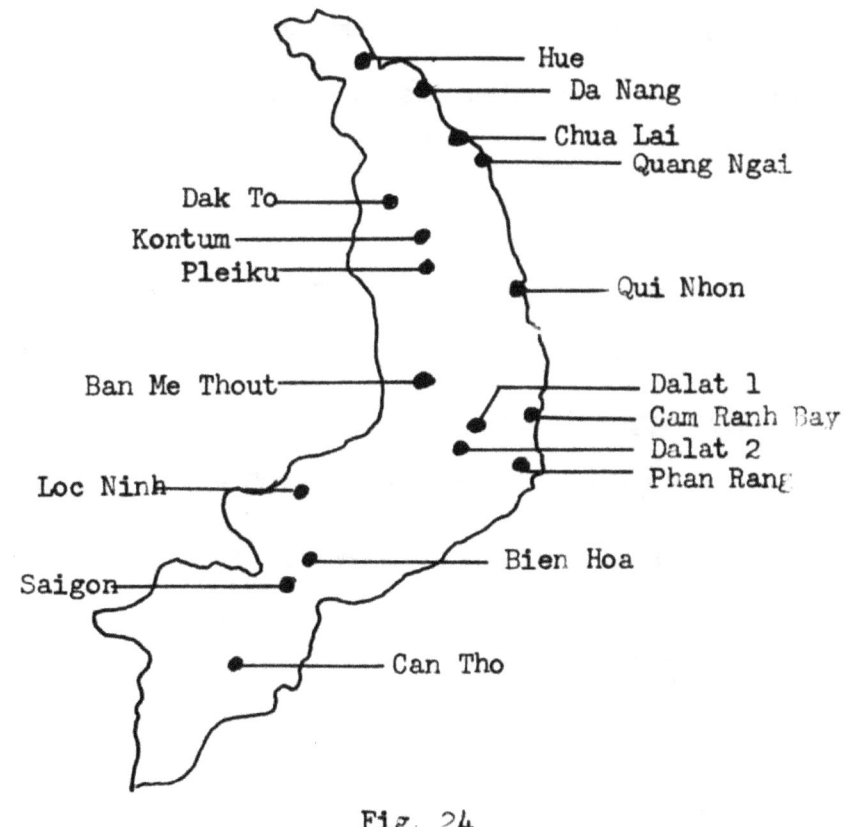

Fig. 24

Many of the tactical airstrips were constructed by the French and were built only for light aircraft operations (C-47 and smaller), designed for 33,000 pounds. The C-130 can, and often does, weigh up to 155,000 pounds. The majority of the airfields used to support the combat units in the field consist only of a runway; taxiways, turnaround areas and parking aprons are inadequate or nonexistent. This allows the airfield to accept only one aircraft at a time.

Airfields without surfaces adequate in area and load bearing capacity to permit normal aircraft ground maneuvering and cargo offloading have serious limitations and are vulnerable to damage by normal aircraft ground operations. The tandem rear wheels of the C-130 drag when the turning radious is reduced. The dragging of these rear wheels digs and cuts ruts in the dirt, rips up membranes, and rips up PSP or aluminum matting. This damage soon renders temporary airfields useless and requires considerable engineer effort to repair the damage. Continued use of the C-130 on badly deteriorated assault-type airfields is resulting in serious aircraft maintenance problems. The entire C-130 fleet in SEA is being plagued by one or more of the following:

        a. Cracks, vertical beam, landing gear (B and E models).
        b. Cracks, wing (E model).
        c. Engine mount structural damage (all).

11. <u>Aerial Port Concept</u>

The USAF has developed the 463L Material Handling Equipment

System, and its use to date indicates great promise. However, this system is not compatible with the Army equipment system. When operating at forward airfields, in practice, Army and Air Force personnel and equipment are utilized jointly to load and unload aircraft. With differences in equipment, procedures, and training, standardization of operations are difficult to obrain. Active aerial port detachments are shown below:

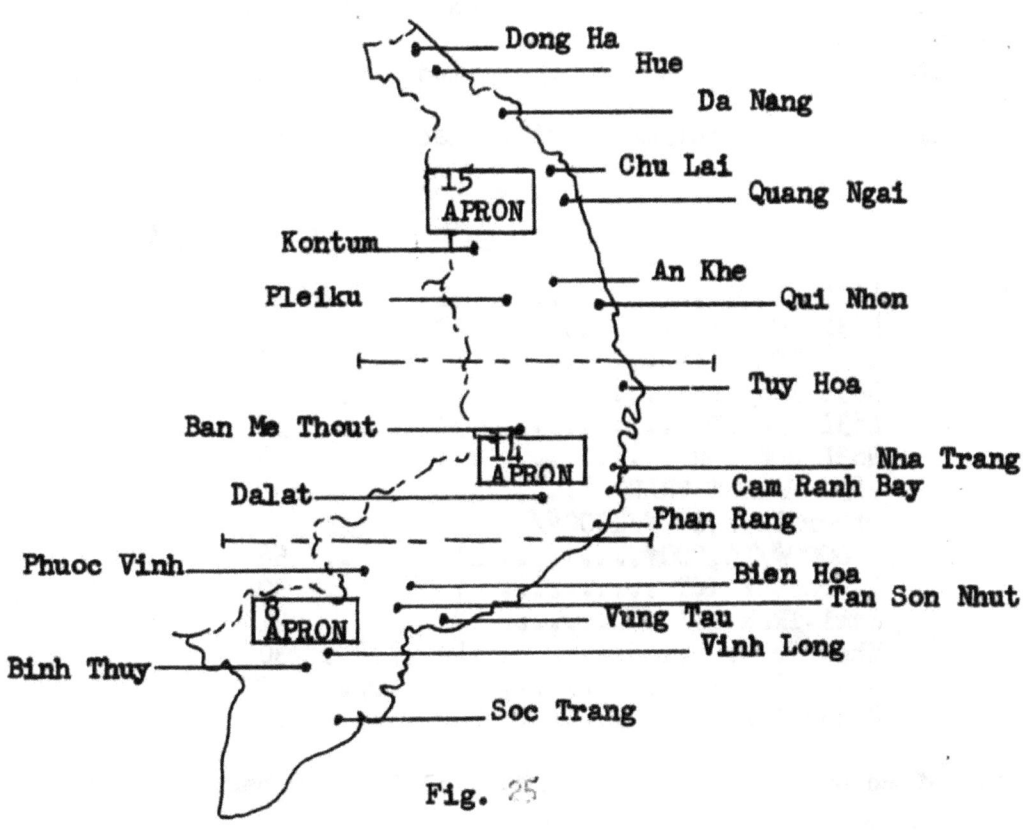

Fig. 25

The operation of an aerial port in support of a major Army unit (division) is a vast undertaking. An example is the 1st Cavalry Division. With a population of approximately 20,000, this unit receives by air approximately 1,800 tons of cargo per month. The present condition of the airfield severely limits air shipment. The R&R (rest and recuperation) program, plus normal rotations require the movement of at least 10,000 passengers per month. This type of workload compares favorably with that of some of the largest permanent type military installations in the CONUS. The Aerial Port Detachment at An Khe, with the 1st Cavalry Division, while performing superbly, is operating under the most primitive conditions. The detachment consisted of four airmen and one borrowed forklift from the Army. One second lieutenant had been assigned and was enroute. Other detachments were conducting operations in similar environments. The Materials Handling Equipment authorized is as follows:

	Auth	On Hand/1 Jun 66
463L 6k FL	41	23
463L 10K FL	72	72
463L 10K RTFL	43	35
463L 10K LDR	14	11
463L 25K LDR	33	31
463L 40K LDR	6	4
463L PALLET TRLR	225	130
Other PL 2,000#/4000#/6000#/16,000#	113	58
T-Tractor IOT	74	30
Semi-TRLR 40'	73	21
Whse Trctr	46	30
Hi-Lift Trk	15	9
General Purpose	102	49

This type of an operation, while perhaps envisioned has not been tested or explored in field tests in the past. A review of the aerial port concept certainly appears necessary. As the capability for airlift improves (45% increase in capability in FY 67, alone), the workload of these units will increase dramatically, as will the dependence of the customer on the airlift system. The present aerial port concept will require more movement of cargo and traffic specialists as the present evolution is proving. Procedures, equipment, and personnel require field tests under the type of conditions prevailing today, with a hard look to the full C-141 C-5 era. The commander of a Joint Tack Force (JTF) or any Joint Command has a vital interest in this aspect of the ALOC as any breakdown will have an immediate and direct effect on his mobility capability. The practice of direct assistance by the Army and Air Force in Vietnam has made the present Aerial Port System work there. The problem is to develop the Command and Control procedures, supporting systems for handling vast quantities of cargo, and management procedures for interface with the logistics agencies. It may very well be that the cooperative and coordinating system is the best; however, the system as exists today in practice in Vietnam has not been tested in joint exercises, and doctrine as such has not been promulgated.

12. <u>Procedures for Emergency Airdrop and Airlift</u>

The mission of the 315th Air Commando Wing is to operate the common user airlift system within Vietnam, referred to as the Southeast Asia Airlift System (SEAAS). This system includes the airlanding and airdrop of personnel and equipment, night illumination missions in support of both ground and air operations, defoliation missions, and emergency air evacuation.

Except for Special Forces, MACV has experienced little requirement for airdrop techniques. The tonnage airdropped by C-123 aircraft during the period March 1965 - May 1966 averaged about 475 to 500 tons per month.

In October 1965, MACV, recognizing the expanding requirements for aerial resupply, specifically requested that the USAF, in collaboration with MACV, establish requirements for aerial drop systems such as LAPES and PLADS. Implementation would provide users in the forward areas an enhanced capability for aerial supply and resupply. A team of experts has recently visited the RVN to study and test a solution to the airdrop requirement; the results of which are not yet available but may be expected soon from either MACV or the Tactical Air Command (TAC). In the interim, MACV has stated, there must be in-being a capability to airdrop 250 short tons a day for 15 days. This tonnage has been derived through experience as being required to resupply an airmobile brigade task force, comprised of three Infantry battalions, an Artillery battalion (105mm), a composite Battery (155/8 in.), an Engineer Platoon, a Helicopter Battalion, an Air Cavalry Troop, and a Field Support Element during moderate contact. ("Moderate contact" has been explained as heavy engagement one day, every three days.) At present, MACV has this capability with organic Army aircraft. After December 1966, when the CV-2 aircraft become Air Force assets, it will become an Air Force responsibility.

Generally, the 315th ACW capability is planned for application three ways - monthly planned on SEA Airlift Schedule; daily frags, special mission requirements, and unplanned on tactical emergency and emergency resupply. The first two categories are routine in nature and are generally based on known requirements. The unplanned is that which is known less than 72 hours in advance. The unplanned always affects the first two categories because, in order to satisfy all requirements, all airlift is committed. Accordingly, any unplanned airlift requirement is satisfied by airlift withdrawn from scheduled or fragged capability.

MACV's standing requirements against the in-country airlift resource shows that seven C-123 and 21 C-130 aircraft are committed on daily schedules, leaving 24 C-123s and eight C-130s available for special or emergency type missions. A typical tactical emergency mission would necessitate the cancellation of four scheduled missions.

In May 1966, there were 248 emergency resupply missions flown. In addition, there were over 75 tactical emergency missions flown. When the special missions performed during May are added it is quite evident all of these missions detract from the desired airlift schedule.

Other missions flown by the 315th Air Commando Wing are illuminating (flare-drop) and spray missions (defoliant). These are shown by sorties flown (C-123 aircraft) and flares expended by month, up to May 1966:

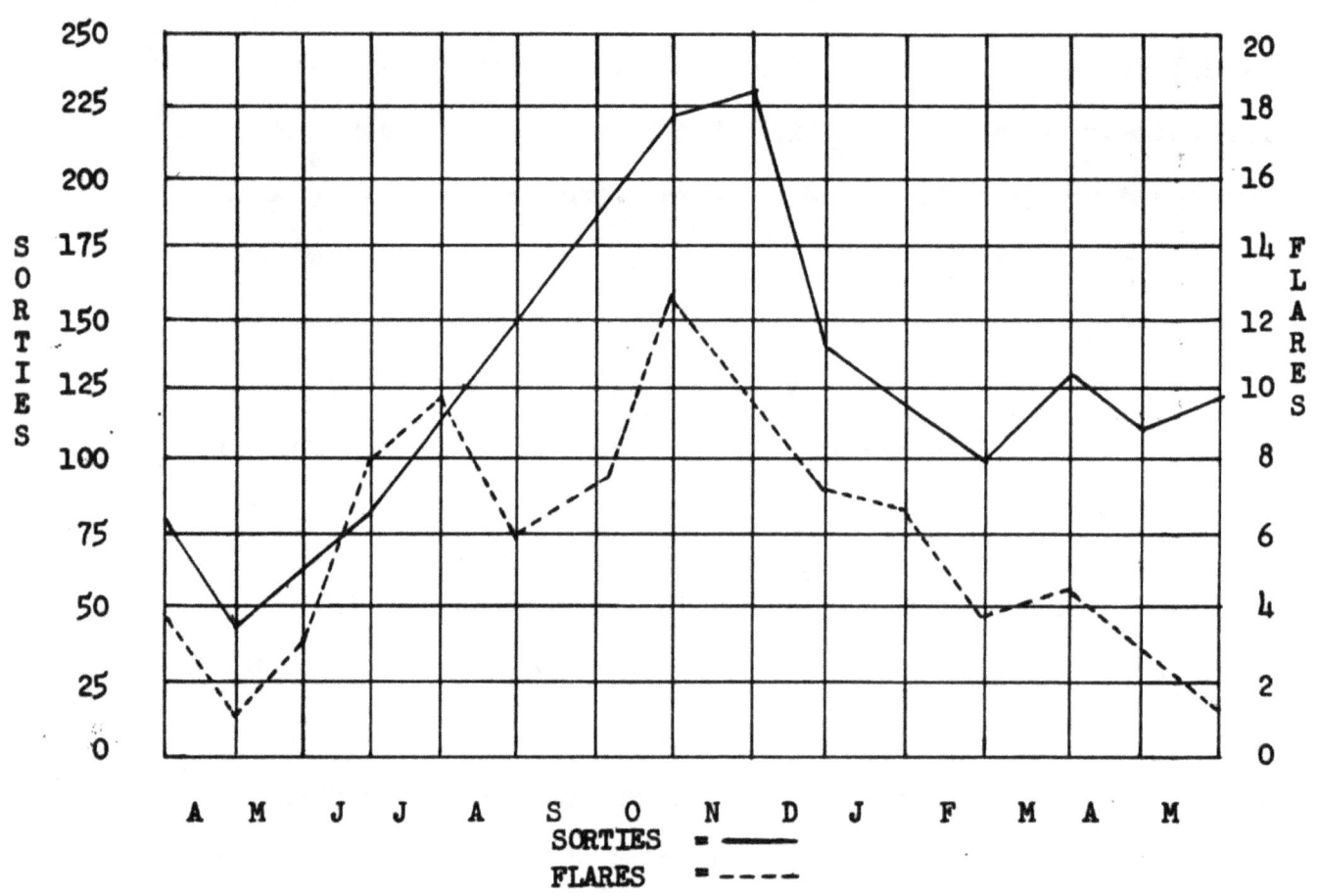

Fig 26

13. <u>Intra-Theater Aeromedical Evacuation</u>

The 9th Aeromedical Evacuation Squadron of the 315th Air Division Tachikawa, Japan, is responsible for the processing and in-flight care of patients. It was planned that, on 8 July 1966, the Squadron would elevate to Group status, with three squadrons located at Tachikawa, Clark, and Tan Son Nhut. Currently, there are 13 detachments in the theater:

Det 2 - Kimpo	Det 9 - Qui Nhon
Det 3 - Kadena	Det 10 - Cam Ranh Bay
Det 4 - Clark	Det 11 - Udorn
Det 5 - Don Muang	Det 12 - Korat
Det 6 - Tan Son Nhut	Det 13 - Ubon
Det 7 - Da Nang	Det 14 - Takhli
Det 8 - Nha Trang	

The majority of the intra-theater patient movements in the tactical phase of evacuation are made by return flights of the 315AD aircraft which have carried troops and cargo to the forward areas. Some of these aircraft are under the operational control of the 315th Air Commando Wing (in-country) and some under direct operational control of the 315AD.

Because of the extensive dispersion of Army medical helicopters and the ability to convert tactical aircraft to aeromedical use as well as the relative short distance between points of origin to initial medical emergency facilities, the bulk of emergency in-country patient movements from battlefield or collecting points is accomplished by the Army.

During the period January-May 1966, a total of 21,487 patients were airlifted; 11,382 flying hours expended; and 14,363 missions flown.

Regulation of patients to available beds and specialty care in off-shore treatment facilities (Guam, Philippines, Okinawa, Japan) is by the MACV surgeon (Medical Regulating Office) and by the Far East Medical Regulating Office in Japan, under the PACOM surgeon. Airframes used are C-118's and C-130's of the 315AD; use of these aircraft for patient movement is arranged through coordination with the detachments of the 9th AME Squadron in-country and off-shore, and the Airlift Control Center (ALCC). Non-scheduled aeromedical flights are classified as Urgent (2-hour requirement), Priority (24-hour requirement), or Routine (72-hour requirement).

Patients destined for further evacuation from off-shore hospitals to the CONUS are transported by MAC C-135 and C-141 type aircraft, reconfigured after cargo and troop hauls from CONUS ports. On 1 July 1966, MAC introduced evacuation service from Tan Son Nhut Airfield, Saigon, to CONUS to stabilized patients requiring medical treatment over the theater limit of 120 days. As air facilities improve in-country to accomodate the C-141 aircraft, additional patients can be evacuated directly from in-country locations.

14. C-130 Shuttle Activity

These aircraft are purely an operational force, with only "as needed" maintenance performed in-country. The aircraft usually fly full loads into the RVN when positioning in-country from their home stations, become part of the shuttle force for a prescribed time, and then redeploy back to their home stations.

Page 114 indicates the accomplishments of this C-130 shuttle force from July 1965 to 30 June 1966. The total weight of cargo and passengers carried per month by this force has increased by an approximate factor of 4.5 since July 1965. The average number of aircraft possessed in-country since January 1966 increased from 32 to 40, and the average operationally ready (O/R) aircraft from 25 to 32. Since January 1966, the utilization rate of the C-130 shuttle force (A, B and E-series aircraft) has averaged 5.3 hours per day, with the average sortie length remaining fairly stable at 46 minutes per sortie as indicated on Page 115. The size of the C-130 shuttle force has surged, at times, to a high of 60 aircraft to satisfy emergency requirements.

PACAF forecasts the number of C-130 shuttle aircraft required through the end of the year will increase to 47.

15. <u>Airlift Aircraft Losses and Battle Damage</u>

As the levels of combat and airlift activity have increased, there has been a corresponding increase in battle damage and attrition to airlift aircraft. The C-123's, particularly, because of their counterinsurgency and defoliant missions, are subject to ground fire. Page 118 depicts the number of aircraft lost and damaged in the RVN from 1962 through July 1966. Since January 1966, more than twice as many C-123 aircraft have been hit by ground fire than both the C-130

113

C-130 SHUTTLE ACTIVITY

Month	Sorties	Flying Time	Avg. Acft Possessed I-C	Avg. Acft Possessed O/R	Cargo	Pax	Short Tons Pax & Cargo	Util Rate Pos'd Acft I-C	Util Rate Pos'd Acft O/R
1965									
Jul	1153	1243	*	*	6,773	18,141	8,950	*	*
Aug	2052	2010	*	*	11,889	20,167	14,309	*	*
Sep	1940	2003	*	*	12,637	19,794	15,012	*	*
Oct	2040	1363*	*	*	12,152	27,575	15,461	*	*
Nov	2997	2591	*	*	15,383	37,998	19,936	*	*
Dec	3792	3350	*	*	20,698	37,497	25,188	*	*
1966									
Jan	5034	4143	32	25	26,189	46,306	31,746	4.2	5.3
Feb	4616	3809	34	28	22,333	46,043	27,372	4.0	4.9
Mar	5734	4595	37	28	29,845	50,702	35,927	4.0	5.3
Apr	7321	5046	41	31	31,822	63,703	38,192	4.1	5.4
May	6973	5182	40	32	31,042	61,958	37,237	4.2	5.2
Jun	7313	5559	40	33	33,365	72,128	40,577	4.6	5.6

Note: I-C = In-country
O/R = Operationally ready
* = Insufficient data

Sources: OPSACT and OPREP 5, Jul-Dec 65 and Aug 1966; 315 ACW Records, Jan-Jul 66.

Fig. 27

C-130 RVN SHUTTLE SUMMARY

	Jan	Feb	Mar	Apr	May	Jun	Jul
Average Aircraft in the RVN	32	34	37	41	40	40	39.5
Average Operationally Ready Acft	25	28	28	31	32	33	32.1
Average Sortie Length	:49	:50	:48	:41	:44	:46	:46
Flying Hours Daily In-Country Acft	4:11	4:00	4:00	4:06	4:11	4:38	4:32
Flying Hours Daily O/R Acft	5:21	4:52	5:17	5:26	5:13	5:37	5:34
Short Tons Per Sortie	6.2	6.0	6.1	5.2	5.3	5.6	5.6
Short Tons Per Flying Hour	7.7	7.2	7.8	7.6	7.2	7.3	7.4
Short Tons Daily O/R Acft	40.0	35.3	40.3	41.0	37.6	41.0	41.2
Short Tons Daily In-Country Acft	31.2	29.0	30.5	31.0	30.0	33.8	33.5

Source: 315th ACW Records, Jan-Jul 66.

Fig 28

C-123 ACTIVITY SUMMARY

	SORTIES FLOWN	PAX CARRIED	CARGO AIRLIFTED
January	5,049	44,119	11,380
February	5,305	37,627	9,869
March	6,632	48,586	12,873
April	6,554	40,125	13,968
May	6,797	44,654	13,804
June	7,619	49,414	15,229
TOTAL (1st half 1966)	37,256	264,525	77,123

Source: Hq PACAF, DOPE Pub. Summary of Air Opns, Vols. I thru XXIV.

Fig. 29

and Army CV-2 combined. Battle damage has been a contributing factor in failure of the C-123 to achieve its programmed flying hour allocation in that maintenance efforts required to repair damage are an additional workload over and above normal maintenance tasks, and the aircraft is out of commission until repaired. While the overall loss rate per 100,000 hours of flying time is relatively low, the impact of the loss of 44 aircraft (19 of which were lost this year) is severe. Of 64 authorized C-123 aircraft, the 315th ACW possessed only 55 during July, while the 315th AD possessed only 162 C-130's of the 192 authorized. Thus, in the case of the PACAF C-130 airlift force, the airlift manager must attempt to satisfy theater airlift requirements with only 84 percent of his authorized force.

Aircraft Availability and Utilization

The degree to which the airlift squadrons possess their authorized aircraft, and the operational readiness of those possessed, are vital to the success of the airlift mission. The C-123 squadrons had difficulty on both counts. With an authorization of 64 airframes (16 per squadron), the average number possessed was 60 in the first quarter of FY 1966, but only 50 in the fourth quarter. The average number operationally ready also declined from 47 (79%)possessed), in the first quarter, to 39 (77%) in the fourth.

Despite the lowered number of airframes available for missions,

AIRCRAFT LOSSES

1 9 6 6

	62-65	Jan	Feb	Mar	Apr	May	Jun	Jul	Total
C-130........	7	2	0	1	0	1	0	0	11
C-123........	18	4	1	0	1	1	2	0	27
CV-2 (USA)...	Not Avail	3	0	0	0	1	0	1	5
Totals....	25	9	1	1	1	3	2	1	43

AIRCRAFT HIT BY GROUND FIRE

	Jan	Feb	Mar	Apr	May	Jun	Jul	Total
C-130...........	3	2	4	15	4	2	2	32
C-123 Airlift...	13	16	12	13	15	13	29	96
C-123 Defoliation	16	24	61	26	30	23	15	230
CV-2 (USA)......	16	15	25	11	20	7	11	105
Totals.......	48	57	102	65	69	45	57	463

Source: NMCC Data & 315th ACW Records

Fig 30

the tons carried per month by the C-123's increased from 16,900 to 19,500 between the first and fourth quarters. This was achieved by flying the ready aircraft one-half hour more per day, and by increasing the tons carried per flying hour by 30%. If more of the authorized aircraft had been possessed and operationally ready, the overall C-123 tonnage could have increased still more.

In-country, the C-130's carried an average of 12,800 tons per month in the first quarter of FY 1966, and 38,700 tons per month in the fourth quarter. Since the average number of tons per flying hour was the same (7.3 tons) in the first and fourth quarters, the increase in total tonnage was achieved by increasing the number of airframes and flying hours.

The C-130 shuttle aircraft belong to the 315th AD. The number of these aircraft authorized to the parent organization increased from 144 in the first quarter to 192 in the fourth, or 33%. However, the average number possessed went up only 12% in the same period, and the average number operationally ready went up only 7%. Thus, the increased accomplishments of the 315AD resulted primarily from a higher number of hours flown per available aircraft rather than from the increase in the number of authorized aircraft. 99/

16. Conclusion

In SEA, classic patterns of deployment and resupply operations do not apply and airlift capability has become a critical factor in carrying out the transportation requirements of the expanded military operation. Experience over the past period shows that the many problem areas stem from lack of communications, loading and parking ramps and knowledge on the part of the airlift users. All have combined to reduce the effectiveness of the SEA Airlift System. Overall average payloads continue to be low, mainly because of the nature of this airlift operation, exigencies of the combat situation, and time-urgency of many cargos. MAC and the 315th Air Division operate over the same routes in some areas, however the strategic/tactical interface is functioning well. Aerial port activity has increased rapidly to extremely high volumes. The port unit resources have never caught up to damands; there continues to be a shortage of personnel, equipment, and facilities. There is an urgent need for a system of developing and updating airlift requirements and a system for challenging individual requests at all levels of command.

Increased use of sealift, both to SEA and intra-coastal RVN, will reduce airlift requirements. Judicious review of priorities and RDD's should reveal an increasing amount of cargo that can be transported in SEA by means other than airlift. By increasing the amount of scheduled airlift in RVN, thereby decreasing the Tactical Emergency, TAC resupply and on-call missions, the overall effectiveness and efficiency of the SEA Airlift System will be increased.

Since approximately 16 percent of the C-130 force is nonproductive due to major maintenance, modifications, battle damage, paintings and corrosion control, an increase in the material and support capability, plus additional C-130 spare aircraft, is required to maintain firm schedules.

Contract passenger flights within the system and additional MAC terminals within the RVN would free more of the airlift fleet for strictly military cargo airlift missions. This would release more of the C-130 fleet to its more effective utilization in hauling large loads for the long-range flights intra and inter-theater. If the C-130J is procured, as requested in February 1966 by CINCPACAF, CINCUSAFE and Commander, Tactical Air Command, then the C-130A can be phased out of the active airlift fleet to the reserve forces and attrition and shortages can be overcome. These commanders at the Tri-Commanders' Conference also indicated that a V/STOL is needed for in-theater flexibility at the terminal end of the ALOC to replace the C-123 fleet. 100/

Based on observation of the conflict in SEA, especially in the RVN, through June 1966, the unreliability of the ground LOC's will remain. The enemy still interdicts these LOC's when he desires. Because of this fact, and the intensified counter-insurgency by the Communists in Thailand, plus the increase in Free World Forces, it appears there will be an increasing requirement for assault airlift in Southeast Asia.

GLOSSARY

AA - Antiaircraft
AB - Air base
ABCCC - Airborne battlefield command and control center
ABG - Airborne battle group
ACG - Air commando group
ACL - Allowable cabin load
ACW - Air commando wing
AD - Air Division
ADVON - Advanced echelon
AF - Air Force (also USAF)
Aeromed - Air medical
ALCC - Airlift control center
ALO - Air liaison officer
APRON - Aerial port squadron (also APS)
ARVN - South Vietnamese Army
ATCO - Airlift traffic coordination office(r)
AVGAS - Aviation gasoline

BLT - Marine battalion landing team

CALSU - Combat airlift support unit
CASF - Combat (composite) air strike force
CC - Combat cargo
CCT - Combat control team
CHMAAG - Chief, Military Advisory Assistance Group
CHWTO - Chief, Western Pacific Transportation Office
CINCPAC - Commander in Chief, Pacific Command
CINCPACAF - Commander in Chief, Pacific Air Forces
CJTF - Chief, Joint Task Force
CONUS - Continental United States

DEFCON - Defense condition
DZ - Drop zone

FIC - French Indo-China
FIW - Fighter-interceptor wing

GPES - Ground proximity extraction system

HF - High frequency

JAAB - Joint Airlift Allocation Board
JCS - Joint Chiefs of Staff
JMTB - Joint Military Transportation Board
JTF - Joint task force

LAPES - Low-altitude parachute extraction system
LOC - Line of communication
LZ - Landing zone

MAAG - Military Advisory Assistance Group
MAC - Military Airlift Command (formerly MATS)
MACV - Military Assistance Command, Vietnam (also COMUSMACV)
MAEG - Medical air evacuation group
MATS - Military Air Transport Service (now MAC)
MCC - Movement control center
MHE - Material handling equipment

Navaid - Navigational aid(s)
NOR - Not operationally ready
NVN - North Vietnam

PACAF - Pacific Air Forces
PACOM - Pacific Area Command
PAX - Passenger(s)
PLADS - Parachute low-altitude delivery system
POL - Petroleum, oil and lubricants
PSP - Pierced steel planking
Psywar - Psychological warfare

RAAF - Royal Australian Air Force
RDD - Required delivery date
RNZAF - Royal New Zealand Air Force
Rote - Rotation(al)
RVN - Republic of Vietnam (South Vietnam)
RVNAF - Royal Vietnamese Air Force (also VNAF)

SEA - Southeast Asia
SEAAS - Southeast Asia Airlift System
SEATO - Southeast Asia Treaty Organization
STOL - Short take-off or landing
SVN - South Vietnam (also RVN)

TAC - Tactical Air Command (also "tactical")
TAC-E - Tactical emergency mission
TACS - Tactical air control system
TCG - Troop carrier group
TCS - Troop carrier squadron
TCW - Troop carrier wing
TDY - Temporary duty
TMA - Traffic Management Agency
TMC - Transport movement control
TRANSPAC - Transpacific
TSN - Tan Son Nhut AB, Saigon, South Vietnam

UHF - Ultra-high frequency

VC - Viet Cong
VFR - Visual flight rules
VNAF - South Vietnamese Air Force (also RVNAF)
VTOL - Vertical take-off or landing

WESTPAC - Western Pacific
WTO - Western Pacific Transportation Office(r)

FOOTNOTES

1/ (S) History, 315ACG, Jul-Dec 64

2/ (S) Special Report, 315AD, 1954

3/ (S) Org Chart, 315 AD, CY 1966

4/ (S) History, 315 AD, Jan-Jun 61

5/ (S) History, 315 AD, Jul Dec 61

6/ (S) Hist Report, 315OC, filed 315 OI-H, Jul-Dec 62

7/ (S) Ibid

8/ (S) Opns Order 226/61, PACAF, 1961

9/ (S) Opns Order 3-62, 315AD, 1962

10/ (S) Opns Order 5-62, 315AD, 1962

11/ (S) See Footnote 6, above

12/ (S) Ibid

13/ (S) Opns Order 6-62, 315AD, 1962

14/ (S) Opns Order 8-62, 315AD, 1962

15/ (S) Opns Order 9-62, 315AD, 1962

16/ (S) See Footnote 6, above

17/ (C) Opns Order 10-62, Hq 315AD, 1962

18/ (C) Opns Order 12-62, Hq 315AD, 1962

19/ (S) See Footnote 15, above

20/ (S) History, 315AD, 1963

21/ (S) Hist Report, 315OC, filed 315 OI-H, Jan-Jun 63

22/ (S) Opns Order 5-63, 315AD, 1963; Ltr, 7APSq, subj: Ex Report, Dhanarahata, dtd 18 Jul 63

23/ (S) See Footnote 21, above

24/ (S) Pub, Stat Summary, PACAF Comptroller, FY 1963

25/ (S) See Footnote 21, above

26/ (S) Ltr, Det 3-315AD to Hq 315AD subj: MCC Cmfrs Report, Gulf of Tonkin Incident, dtd 31 Aug 64.

27/ (S) Pub, Hq USAF, subj: Analysis of SEA Airlift Operations, dtd Sept 66.

28/ (S) Ibid

29/ (S) Ibid

30/ (S) Ibid

31/ (S) Ibid

32/ (S) Ibid

33/ (S) Ibid

34/ (S) Report, USAF Airlift Staff Visit to PACOM 11 Oct-10 Nov 65 (hereinafter referred to as USAF Airlift Report).

35/ (S) History, 2AD, Jan-Jun 65

36/ (S) S.O. G-180, PACAF, 8 Nov 65

37/ (S) S.O. G-215, PACAF, 1 Dec 65

38/ (S) S.O. G-225, PACAF, 15 Dec 65

39/ (S) USAF Airlift Report

40/ (S) Msg, CINCPACAF to 315AD, DPL 52440, quotes CSAF Msg AFCAV 89770, Nov 65

41/ (S) S.O. G-100, PACAF, 8 Aug 65

42/ (S) S.O. G-180, PACAF, 8 Nov 65

43/ (C) Msg, CINCPACAF, DOOT 38961, 18 Nov 65

44/ (S) USAF Airlift Report

45/ (S) Ibid

46/ (S) History, 315AD, p 27, Jul-Dec 65

47/ (S) USAF Airlift Report

48/ (S) Ibid

49/ (S) Msg, 315AD to CINCPAC, 315DO 02390, Nov 65

50/ (S) Msg, 315AD to 463TCW, PAFOP 315DOC 02484, Dec 65

51/ (U) Msg, C-130 CALSU TSN to 315AD, CALSU 43, 22 Dec 65

52/ (U) Msg, C-130 CALSU TSN to CINCPACAF, CALSU 42, 22 Dec 65

53/ (S) Spcl Report, 315AD, subj: Airlift Accomplishments, CY 1965

54/ (S) Pub, USAF, subj: Analysis of SEA Airlift Operations, dtd Sep 66

55/ (S) Msg, 315ACG to 315AD, 315GCR 08066, Oct 65

56/ (S) Msg, CINCPACAF to 315AD, SPECAT AFEO DOCO 34286, Nov 65

57/ (S) Msg, 315AD to all Sub Units, SPECAT AFEO 315DOSS 02430, 2 Dec 65.

58/ (C) Ltr, 315AD to 6315 Ops Gp, 315DOSS, 21 Dec 65

59/ (S) Msg, 6315 Ops Gp to 315AD, SPECAT AFEO 6315GOC 02212, 6 Dec 65

60/ (S) History, 315AD, Jul-Dec 65

61/ (S) Ibid

62/ (S) Ibid

63/ (S) Msg, CINCPACAF to 2AD, subj: Airdrop Dely, dtd Nov 65

64/ (S) Ltr, 2AD to MACV, subj: Airstrip Improvement, dtd Nov 65

65/ (S) Msg, CINCPACAF, SPECAT AFEO DPL 54505, Dec 65

66/ (U) Msg, 2AD to CSAF, IGSA 00702, 18 Dec 65

67/ (S) USAF Airlift Report

68/ (S) Report, subj: Major Aircraft Accidents, files Hq USAF, Norton AFB, Calif

69/ (S) USAF Airlift Report

70/ (S) Ibid

71/ (S) Ibid

72/ (C) Msg, CSAF to PACAF, AFRDQRA - I 77225, 9 Dec 65

73/ (U) Ltr, Col Mataxis to Gen Moore, 19 Aug 65

74/ (S) USAF Airlift Report

75/ (C) Msg, 315AD to CINCPACAF, 02390, Nov 65

76/ (U) Report, AFGOA, subj: Analysis of SEA Airlift Operations, Second Progress Report, dtd May 66

77/ (S) Briefing, WTOB, 26 Apr 66

78/ (TS) Msg, Extract of TS Msg PACAF to CINCPAC, DPLTSC 50/07 Jun 66

79/ (U) See Footnote 77, above

80/ (S) Pub, 315ACW Accomplishment Book, undtd

81/ (U) See Footnote 77, above

82/ (C) Msg, WTO to COMUSMACV, PAFOP WTO 0229, Aug 66

83/ (S) Msg, PACAF, DOP 52259, 22 May 66

84/ (S) Msg, 315AD, DOP 02080, 23 May 66

85/ (S) Msg, CSAF, AFXPD 91625, 24 May 66

86/ (S) Msg, TAC DO 57548, 26 May 66

87/ (TS) See Footnote 78, above

88/ (U) See Footnote 76, above

89/ (S) NMCC Data & 315 ACW Records

90/ (S) Historical Summary, Dep of AF Advisory Group, Mar 66

91/ (TS) Pub, Tri-Commanders' Conference Book, PACAF, USAF, TAC, 8-9 Feb 66

92/ (S) Msg, PACAF to CINCPAC, 52776, Jun 66

93/ (U) See Footnote 76, above

94/ (S) Ltr, subj: C-130 In-Country Operations, 6 Aug 66

95/ (C) Msg, 315ACW to 315AD, FASTEL, subj: J-38 Report, 66

96/ (S) See Footnote 77, above

97/ (U) See Footnote 76, above

98/ (S) Pub, Hq USAF, subj: Analysis of SEA Airlift Operations, dtd Sep 66

99/ (S) Ibid

100/ (TS) See Footnote 91, above

www.ingramcontent.com/pod-product-compliance
Lightning Source LLC
Chambersburg PA
CBHW080549170426
43195CB00016B/2730